This planner belongs to:

_____

_____

_____

BE THE DIFFERENCE MONTHLY PLANNER

ISBN 978-0-593-23528-7

Copyright © 2021 by WaterBrook
Design by Danielle Deschenes, Jessie Kaye, and Nicole Block
Illustrations by Chantell Marlowe
Icons on pages 20-21, 30-31, 40-41, 54-55, 64-65, 74-75, 88-89, 98-99, 108-109, 122-123, 132-133, 142-143 © Shutterstock.com / miniwide
Sun icon © Shutterstock.com / miniwide
Smiley face icons © Shutterstock.com / roroto12p

Published in the United States by WaterBrook, an imprint of Random House, a division of Penguin Random House.

Ink & Willow and its colophon are registered trademarks of Penguin Random House LLC.

Printed in Thailand

2022—First Edition

10 9 8 7 6 5 4 3 2 1

SPECIAL SALES
Most WaterBrook and Ink & Willow books are available at special quantity discounts when purchased in bulk by corporations, organizations, and special-interest groups. Custom imprinting or excerpting can also be done to fit special needs. For information, please e-mail specialmarketscms@penguinrandomhouse.com.

BE THE DIFFERENCE

MONTHLY PLANNER

Serve Others and Change the World

Ink &
Willow

INTRODUCTION

He has told you, O man, what is good;
and what does the Lord require of you
but to do justice, and to love kindness,
and to walk humbly with your God?
— MICAH 6:8 (ESV)

The world around us has always been broken, but as believers, we have been called to do something about it. In fact, when Jesus walked on earth, caring for the poor, the widows, the orphans, and the marginalized was a major part of His ministry. He saw and recognized the broken parts of the world, but rather than just shrugging them off in a "that's just the way the world is" kind of way, He chose to act.

If you picked up this planner, chances are you probably feel a similar urge to help restore and repair the world's broken parts. You want to change the world, but when it comes to deciding what issue(s) to focus on or even where to begin, you feel a bit lost. You wouldn't call yourself an activist, but you still want to . . . well . . . *act*. Do something. Make a difference.

To avoid feeling overwhelmed or disillusioned when facing such an important undertaking, the trick is to take things one month, one week, and one day at a time, and that's where the *Be the Difference Planner* can help. Within these pages, you'll find the space and tools to identify the issues that matter most to you and to help you map out intentional steps to create a meaningful impact.

Whether you choose to focus on one issue month after month, or you choose to rotate through issues, the Bible says that "each one of you should use whatever gift you have received to serve others, as faithful stewards of God's grace in its various forms" (1 Peter 4:10).

THIS PLANNER WILL GUIDE YOU THROUGH KEY STEPS:

- doing the research and growing your awareness about specific causes locally, nationally, and globally;

- finding and connecting with a like-minded community;

- strengthening your advocacy skills by learning how to maximize your time, talents, resources, and voice.

As a person of faith, you probably believe that God can create beauty even from the most lifeless ashes and make all things new. Redemption is part of His plan, and the amazing thing is that He has called us to be a part of it. By using this planner, you're taking the first step.

Within the first pages of this planner, you are invited to write, sketch, or cut and paste images about the issues that matter most to you. Of course, there are so many causes to choose from, and narrowing your focus can feel impossibly overwhelming, but this space has been designed to help you identify the best starting point based on your personal passions and how your talents and skills can help you advocate well. If you're still feeling stuck, the back of this planner has an overview of some major issues along with lists of both faith-based and mainstream organizations that are already doing the work.

At the beginning of each month, you will have the freedom to choose a specific cause or issue to focus on from your brainstorming pages. The next month, you can choose to focus on the same issue or explore a new cause to champion. You will be challenged to do research, find a community to connect or get involved with, and set specific goals around how you can use your voice or resources to have immediate impact locally, nationally, or globally.

At the end of each month, you will have space to reflect on your progress, what you have learned, or whether you need to make any adjustments in your advocacy.

You'll also find space to organize your month in a way that works best for you. Each month, you can set a new goal, such as researching, volunteering, relationship building, or self-care, with room to jot down key takeaways and insights from each week. You can look back at these notes when you reflect at the end of each month.

In addition to the monthly spreads, this planner features bonus content for diving deeper into your advocacy journey.

Voices
TO FOLLOW

READ/ WATCH/ LISTEN *Lists*

Advocate **PROFILES**

Project **PLANNERS**

REFLECT AND RESET *Check-ins*

Places **TO VISIT**

Overview **OF CURRENT MAIN ISSUES**

GIVING AND DONATION *Tracker*

CONTACTS

Feel free to use as many (or as few) of the prompts and spaces as are useful for you. This planner is meant to be curated according to your own personality, preferences, and passions. Make it your own!

NOW GO OUT AND BE THE DIFFERENCE AS YOU SERVE OTHERS AND CHANGE THE WORLD.

2022   2023   2024

2022

JANUARY
S	M	T	W	T	F	S
						1
2	3	4	5	6	7	8
9	10	11	12	13	14	15
16	17	18	19	20	21	22
23	24	25	26	27	28	29
30	31					

FEBRUARY
S	M	T	W	T	F	S
		1	2	3	4	5
6	7	8	9	10	11	12
13	14	15	16	17	18	19
20	21	22	23	24	25	26
27	28					

MARCH
S	M	T	W	T	F	S
		1	2	3	4	5
6	7	8	9	10	11	12
13	14	15	16	17	18	19
20	21	22	23	24	25	26
27	28	29	30	31		

APRIL
S	M	T	W	T	F	S
					1	2
3	4	5	6	7	8	9
10	11	12	13	14	15	16
17	18	19	20	21	22	23
24	25	26	27	28	29	30

MAY
S	M	T	W	T	F	S
1	2	3	4	5	6	7
8	9	10	11	12	13	14
15	16	17	18	19	20	21
22	23	24	25	26	27	28
29	30					

JUNE
S	M	T	W	T	F	S
			1	2	3	4
5	6	7	8	9	10	11
12	13	14	15	16	17	18
19	20	21	22	23	24	25
26	27	28	29	30		

JULY
S	M	T	W	T	F	S
					1	2
3	4	5	6	7	8	9
10	11	12	13	14	15	16
17	18	19	20	21	22	23
24	25	26	27	28	29	30
31						

AUGUST
S	M	T	W	T	F	S
	1	2	3	4	5	6
7	8	9	10	11	12	13
14	15	16	17	18	19	20
21	22	23	24	25	26	27
28	29	30	31			

SEPTEMBER
S	M	T	W	T	F	S
				1	2	
3	4	5	6	7	8	9
10	11	12	13	14	15	16
17	18	19	20	21	22	23
24	25	26	27	28	29	30

OCTOBER
S	M	T	W	T	F	S
						1
2	3	4	5	6	7	8
9	10	11	12	13	14	15
16	17	18	19	20	21	22
23	24	25	26	27	28	29
30	31					

NOVEMBER
S	M	T	W	T	F	S
		1	2	3	4	5
6	7	8	9	10	11	12
13	14	15	16	17	18	19
20	21	22	23	24	25	26
27	28	29	30			

DECEMBER
S	M	T	W	T	F	S
				1	2	3
4	5	6	7	8	9	10
11	12	13	14	15	16	17
18	19	20	21	22	23	24
25	26	27	28	29	30	31

2023

JANUARY
S	M	T	W	T	F	S
1	2	3	4	5	6	7
8	9	10	11	12	13	14
15	16	17	18	19	20	21
22	23	24	25	26	27	28
29	30	31				

FEBRUARY
S	M	T	W	T	F	S
			1	2	3	4
5	6	7	8	9	10	11
12	13	14	15	16	17	18
19	20	21	22	23	24	25
26	27	28				

MARCH
S	M	T	W	T	F	S
			1	2	3	4
5	6	7	8	9	10	11
12	13	14	15	16	17	18
19	20	21	22	23	24	25
26	27	28	29	30	31	

APRIL
S	M	T	W	T	F	S
						1
2	3	4	5	6	7	8
9	10	11	12	13	14	15
16	17	18	19	20	21	22
23	24	25	26	27	28	29
30						

MAY
S	M	T	W	T	F	S
	1	2	3	4	5	6
7	8	9	10	11	12	13
14	15	16	17	18	19	20
21	22	23	24	25	26	27
28	29	30	31			

JUNE
S	M	T	W	T	F	S
				1	2	3
4	5	6	7	8	9	10
11	12	13	14	15	16	17
18	19	20	21	22	23	24
25	26	27	28	29	30	

JULY
S	M	T	W	T	F	S
						1
2	3	4	5	6	7	8
9	10	11	12	13	14	15
16	17	18	19	20	21	22
23	24	25	26	27	28	29
30	31					

AUGUST
S	M	T	W	T	F	S
		1	2	3	4	5
6	7	8	9	10	11	12
13	14	15	16	17	18	19
20	21	22	23	24	25	26
27	28	29	30	31		

SEPTEMBER
S	M	T	W	T	F	S
					1	2
3	4	5	6	7	8	9
10	11	12	13	14	15	16
17	18	19	20	21	22	23
24	25	26	27	28	29	30

OCTOBER
S	M	T	W	T	F	S
1	2	3	4	5	6	7
8	9	10	11	12	13	14
15	16	17	18	19	20	21
22	23	24	25	26	27	28
29	30	31				

NOVEMBER
S	M	T	W	T	F	S
			1	2	3	4
5	6	7	8	9	10	11
12	13	14	15	16	17	18
19	20	21	22	23	24	25
26	27	28	29	30		

DECEMBER
S	M	T	W	T	F	S
					1	2
3	4	5	6	7	8	9
10	11	12	13	14	15	16
17	18	19	20	21	22	23
24	25	26	27	28	29	30
31						

2024

JANUARY
S	M	T	W	T	F	S
	1	2	3	4	5	6
7	8	9	10	11	12	13
14	15	16	17	18	19	20
21	22	23	24	25	26	27
28	29	30	31			

FEBRUARY
S	M	T	W	T	F	S
				1	2	3
4	5	6	7	8	9	10
11	12	13	14	15	16	17
18	19	20	21	22	23	24
25	26	27	28	29		

MARCH
S	M	T	W	T	F	S
					1	2
3	4	5	6	7	8	9
10	11	12	13	14	15	16
17	18	19	20	21	22	23
24	25	26	27	28	29	30
31						

APRIL
S	M	T	W	T	F	S
	1	2	3	4	5	6
7	8	9	10	11	12	13
14	15	16	17	18	19	20
21	22	23	24	25	26	27
28	29	30				

MAY
S	M	T	W	T	F	S
			1	2	3	4
5	6	7	8	9	10	11
12	13	14	15	16	17	18
19	20	21	22	23	24	25
26	27	28	29	30	31	

JUNE
S	M	T	W	T	F	S
						1
2	3	4	5	6	7	8
9	10	11	12	13	14	15
16	17	18	19	20	21	22
23	24	25	26	27	28	29
30						

JULY
S	M	T	W	T	F	S
	1	2	3	4	5	6
7	8	9	10	11	12	13
14	15	16	17	18	19	20
21	22	23	24	25	26	27
28	29	30	31			

AUGUST
S	M	T	W	T	F	S
				1	2	3
4	5	6	7	8	9	10
11	12	13	14	15	16	17
18	19	20	21	22	23	24
25	26	27	28	29	30	31

SEPTEMBER
S	M	T	W	T	F	S
1	2	3	4	5	6	7
8	9	10	11	12	13	14
15	16	17	18	19	20	21
22	23	24	25	26	27	28
29	30					

OCTOBER
S	M	T	W	T	F	S
		1	2	3	4	5
6	7	8	9	10	11	12
13	14	15	16	17	18	19
20	21	22	23	24	25	26
27	28	29	30	31		

NOVEMBER
S	M	T	W	T	F	S
					1	2
3	4	5	6	7	8	9
10	11	12	13	14	15	16
17	18	19	20	21	22	23
24	25	26	27	28	29	30

DECEMBER
S	M	T	W	T	F	S
1	2	3	4	5	6	7
8	9	10	11	12	13	14
15	16	17	18	19	20	21
22	23	24	25	26	27	28
29	30	31				

2025

JANUARY
S	M	T	W	T	F	S
			1	2	3	4
5	6	7	8	9	10	11
12	13	14	15	16	17	18
19	20	21	22	23	24	25
26	27	28	29	30	31	

FEBRUARY
S	M	T	W	T	F	S
						1
2	3	4	5	6	7	8
9	10	11	12	13	14	15
16	17	18	19	20	21	22
23	24	25	26	27	28	

MARCH
S	M	T	W	T	F	S
						1
2	3	4	5	6	7	8
9	10	11	12	13	14	15
16	17	18	19	20	21	22
23	24	25	26	27	28	29
30	31					

APRIL
S	M	T	W	T	F	S
		1	2	3	4	5
6	7	8	9	10	11	12
13	14	15	16	17	18	19
20	21	22	23	24	25	26
27	28	29	30			

MAY
S	M	T	W	T	F	S
				1	2	3
4	5	6	7	8	9	10
11	12	13	14	15	16	17
18	19	20	21	22	23	24
25	26	27	28	29	30	31

JUNE
S	M	T	W	T	F	S
1	2	3	4	5	6	7
8	9	10	11	12	13	14
15	16	17	18	19	20	21
22	23	24	25	26	27	28
29	30					

JULY
S	M	T	W	T	F	S
		1	2	3	4	5
6	7	8	9	10	11	12
13	14	15	16	17	18	19
20	21	22	23	24	25	26
27	28	29	30	31		

AUGUST
S	M	T	W	T	F	S
					1	2
3	4	5	6	7	8	9
10	11	12	13	14	15	16
17	18	19	20	21	22	23
24	25	26	27	28	29	30
31						

SEPTEMBER
S	M	T	W	T	F	S
	1	2	3	4	5	6
7	8	9	10	11	12	13
14	15	16	17	18	19	20
21	22	23	24	25	26	27
28	29	30				

OCTOBER
S	M	T	W	T	F	S
			1	2	3	4
5	6	7	8	9	10	11
12	13	14	15	16	17	18
19	20	21	22	23	24	25
26	27	28	29	30	31	

NOVEMBER
S	M	T	W	T	F	S
						1
2	3	4	5	6	7	8
9	10	11	12	13	14	15
16	17	18	19	20	21	22
23	24	25	26	27	28	29
30						

DECEMBER
S	M	T	W	T	F	S
	1	2	3	4	5	6
7	8	9	10	11	12	13
14	15	16	17	18	19	20
21	22	23	24	25	26	27
28	29	30	31			

2026

JANUARY
S	M	T	W	T	F	S
				1	2	3
4	5	6	7	8	9	10
11	12	13	14	15	16	17
18	19	20	21	22	23	24
25	26	27	28	29	30	31

FEBRUARY
S	M	T	W	T	F	S
1	2	3	4	5	6	7
8	9	10	11	12	13	14
15	16	17	18	19	20	21
22	23	24	25	26	27	28

MARCH
S	M	T	W	T	F	S
1	2	3	4	5	6	7
8	9	10	11	12	13	14
15	16	17	18	19	20	21
22	23	24	25	26	27	28
29	30	31				

APRIL
S	M	T	W	T	F	S
			1	2	3	4
5	6	7	8	9	10	11
12	13	14	15	16	17	18
19	20	21	22	23	24	25
26	27	28	29	30		

MAY
S	M	T	W	T	F	S
					1	2
3	4	5	6	7	8	9
10	11	12	13	14	15	16
17	18	19	20	21	22	23
24	25	26	27	28	29	30
31						

JUNE
S	M	T	W	T	F	S
	1	2	3	4	5	6
7	8	9	10	11	12	13
14	15	16	17	18	19	20
21	22	23	24	25	26	27
28	29	30				

JULY
S	M	T	W	T	F	S
			1	2	3	4
5	6	7	8	9	10	11
12	13	14	15	16	17	18
19	20	21	22	23	24	25
26	27	28	29	30	31	

AUGUST
S	M	T	W	T	F	S
						1
2	3	4	5	6	7	8
9	10	11	12	13	14	15
16	17	18	19	20	21	22
23	24	25	26	27	28	29
30	31					

SEPTEMBER
S	M	T	W	T	F	S
		1	2	3	4	5
6	7	8	9	10	11	12
13	14	15	16	17	18	19
20	21	22	23	24	25	26
27	28	29	30			

OCTOBER
S	M	T	W	T	F	S
				1	2	3
4	5	6	7	8	9	10
11	12	13	14	15	16	17
18	19	20	21	22	23	24
25	26	27	28	29	30	31

NOVEMBER
S	M	T	W	T	F	S
1	2	3	4	5	6	7
8	9	10	11	12	13	14
15	16	17	18	19	20	21
22	23	24	25	26	27	28
29	30					

DECEMBER
S	M	T	W	T	F	S
		1	2	3	4	5
6	7	8	9	10	11	12
13	14	15	16	17	18	19
20	21	22	23	24	25	26
27	28	29	30	31		

2027

JANUARY
S	M	T	W	T	F	S
					1	2
3	4	5	6	7	8	9
10	11	12	13	14	15	16
17	18	19	20	21	22	23
24	25	26	27	28	29	30
31						

FEBRUARY
S	M	T	W	T	F	S
	1	2	3	4	5	6
7	8	9	10	11	12	13
14	15	16	17	18	19	20
21	22	23	24	25	26	27
28						

MARCH
S	M	T	W	T	F	S
	1	2	3	4	5	6
7	8	9	10	11	12	13
14	15	16	17	18	19	20
21	22	23	24	25	26	27
28	29	30	31			

APRIL
S	M	T	W	T	F	S
				1	2	3
4	5	6	7	8	9	10
11	12	13	14	15	16	17
18	19	20	21	22	23	24
25	26	27	28	29	30	

MAY
S	M	T	W	T	F	S
						1
2	3	4	5	6	7	8
9	10	11	12	13	14	15
16	17	18	19	20	21	22
23	24	25	26	27	28	29
30	31					

JUNE
S	M	T	W	T	F	S
		1	2	3	4	5
6	7	8	9	10	11	12
13	14	15	16	17	18	19
20	21	22	23	24	25	26
27	28	29	30			

JULY
S	M	T	W	T	F	S
				1	2	3
4	5	6	7	8	9	10
11	12	13	14	15	16	17
18	19	20	21	22	23	24
25	26	27	28	29	30	31

AUGUST
S	M	T	W	T	F	S
1	2	3	4	5	6	7
8	9	10	11	12	13	14
15	16	17	18	19	20	21
22	23	24	25	26	27	28
29	30	31				

SEPTEMBER
S	M	T	W	T	F	S
			1	2	3	4
5	6	7	8	9	10	11
12	13	14	15	16	17	18
19	20	21	22	23	24	25
26	27	28	29	30		

OCTOBER
S	M	T	W	T	F	S
					1	2
3	4	5	6	7	8	9
10	11	12	13	14	15	16
17	18	19	20	21	22	23
24	25	26	27	28	29	30
31						

NOVEMBER
S	M	T	W	T	F	S
	1	2	3	4	5	6
7	8	9	10	11	12	13
14	15	16	17	18	19	20
21	22	23	24	25	26	27
28	29	30				

DECEMBER
S	M	T	W	T	F	S
			1	2	3	4
5	6	7	8	9	10	11
12	13	14	15	16	17	18
19	20	21	22	23	24	25
26	27	28	29	30	31	

WHAT MATTERS
to Me

Don't look for big things, just do small things with great love. The smaller the thing, the greater must be our love.
— MOTHER TERESA

CAUSES AND ISSUES THAT MATTER TO ME:

- racial reconciliation
- gender equality
- poverty
- world hunger
- immigration
- refugee crisis
- Green Earth
- sustainability
- international relations
- clean water
- adoption
- fostering
- _____
- _____
- _____
- _____
- _____

ORGANIZATIONS I ADMIRE OR PEOPLE WHO ARE INFLUENTIAL IN THESE SPACES:

- ○ _____
- ○ _____
- ○ _____
- ○ _____
- ○ _____
- ○ _____
- ○ _____
- ○ _____
- ○ _____
- ○ _____

SOME ISSUES THAT CONCERN ME THE MOST IN THE FOLLOWING AREAS:

LOCALLY	NATIONALLY	GLOBALLY

IF I COULD CHANGE ANYTHING IN THE WORLD OVERNIGHT, IT WOULD BE:

_____

_____

_____

_____

Where I COME IN

RIGHT NOW I'M ESPECIALLY PASSIONATE ABOUT:

_____

_____

_____

_____

_____

_____

_____

_____

_____

_____

_____

WORDS TO DESCRIBE ME:

- ✖ researcher
- ✖ organizer
- ✖ leader
- ✖ advocate
- ✖ _____
- ✖ _____
- ✖ _____
- ✖ _____
- ✖ _____
- ✖ _____

MY STRENGTHS:

- ✖ empathy
- ✖ helpfulness
- ✖ determination
- ✖ confidence
- ✖ loyalty
- ✖ patience

- ✖ kindness
- ✖ generosity
- ✖ amiability
- ✖ selflessness
- ✖ energy
- ✖ humor

- ✖ relatability
- ✖ personableness
- ✖ positivity
- ✖ realism
- ✖ idealism
- ✖ _____

CAUSES I'VE CHAMPIONED IN THE PAST:

_____

_____

_____

_____

_____

_____

_____

How I Feel About
MY ADVOCACY RIGHT NOW

awesome | 10

9

8

7

6

5

4

3

2

needs work | 1

CHARACTERISTICS I WOULD LIKE TO CULTIVATE OR FOCUS ON IN MYSELF:

MY SPHERES OF INFLUENCE:

- home
- family
- friends
- church
- school
- job
- volunteer organizations
- association board
- _____
- _____
- _____
- _____

My Advocacy VISION BOARD

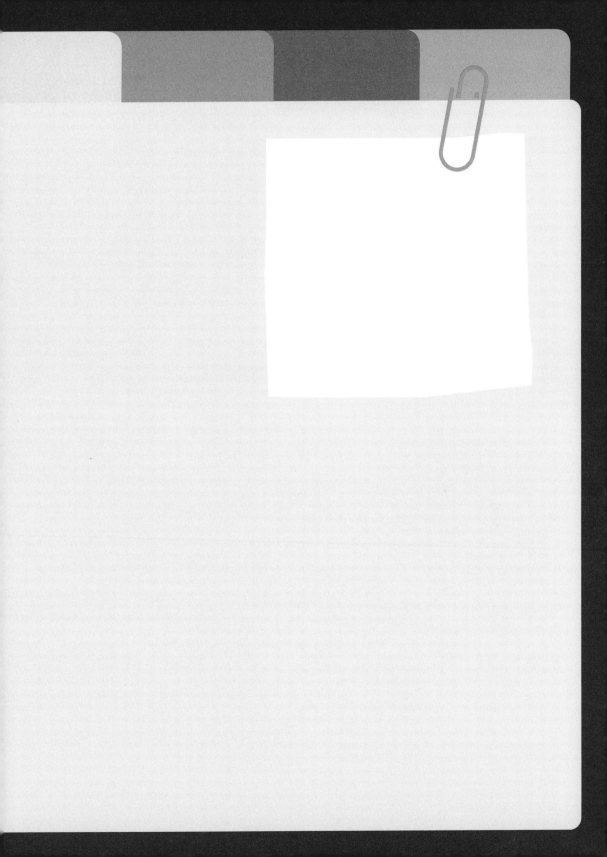

THINKING
THROUGH
the PROBLEM

As you seek to make a difference in specific areas, use this creative problem-solving process to guide you in breaking down big issues into manageable action steps. This is not a linear process, and you may have to repeat certain steps to refine your ideas and make greater impact.

EMPATHIZE

How can I see from the perspective of the people affected by the issues?

DEFINE PROBLEM(S)

What are some of the underlying causes behind this issue?

BRAINSTORM SOLUTIONS

What are practical ways I can make a difference? (Think big/bold and small/simple.)

TAKE ACTION

How can I implement
my idea in the real
world? Who can I bring
on board to help?

GET FEEDBACK

What do others think
of my idea? Are there
any changes I can
incorporate?

PLAN STEPS

What steps can I take
to make my ideas come
to life? Who can I engage
to come alongside me?

Monday	Tuesday	Wednesday	Thursday

Whoever is kind to the poor lends to the Lord, and he will reward them for what they have done.   — PROVERBS 19:17

Friday	Saturday	Sunday

MISSION FOR THE MONTH:

_____

_____

_____

_____

_____

THREE ITEMS TO RESEARCH RELATED TO MY MISSION:

_____

_____

_____

TASKS TO FOCUS ON:

_____

_____

_____

_____

_____

_____

_____

ADVOCACY ACTION ITEMS
for the Month

Create practical action steps you plan to take to help you meet the mission you have chosen to focus on this month. Fill out as many or as few of the categories as you would like to commit to.

WAYS I CAN ADVOCATE WITH MY . . .
(circle one)

 Time   Talents   Resources   Voice

_____

_____

_____

WAYS I CAN ADVOCATE WITH MY . . .
(circle one)

 Time   Talents   Resources   Voice

_____

_____

_____

GLOBAL

WAYS I CAN ADVOCATE WITH MY . . .

(circle one)

Time

Talents

Resources

Voice

_____

_____

_____

NOTES

_____

_____

_____

_____

_____

_____

_____

MONTH:

_____

PEOPLE/ORGANIZATIONS
TO CONNECT WITH

○ _____

○ _____

○ _____

○ _____

○ _____

VOICES TO FOLLOW

(any authors, influencers, organizations, politicians, activists, etc. I already follow or would like to learn more about)

✗ _____

✗ _____

✗ _____

✗ _____

✗ _____

✗ _____

✗ _____

PRAYER REQUESTS

SELF-CARE

(Remember to rest and recharge. Advocacy work can be hard!)

TO-DOS FOR EACH WEEK

NOTES

This Month's
READ/WATCH/ LISTEN LIST

MONTH:

_____

Record any media you read, watch, or listen to this month and reflect on key takeaways or quotes you would like to remember.

Date: _____ Rating: ☆ ☆ ☆ ☆ ☆

Title: _____

Source/Author: _____

What I learned: _____

_____

What surprised me: _____

_____

Memorable quote: _____

_____

Date: _____ Rating: ☆ ☆ ☆ ☆ ☆

Title: _____

Source/Author: _____

What I learned: _____

_____

What surprised me: _____

_____

Memorable quote: _____

_____

Date: _____ Rating: ☆ ☆ ☆ ☆ ☆

Title: _____

Source/Author: _____

What I learned: _____

_____

What surprised me: _____

_____

Memorable quote: _____

_____

REFLECTING
on the PAST MONTH

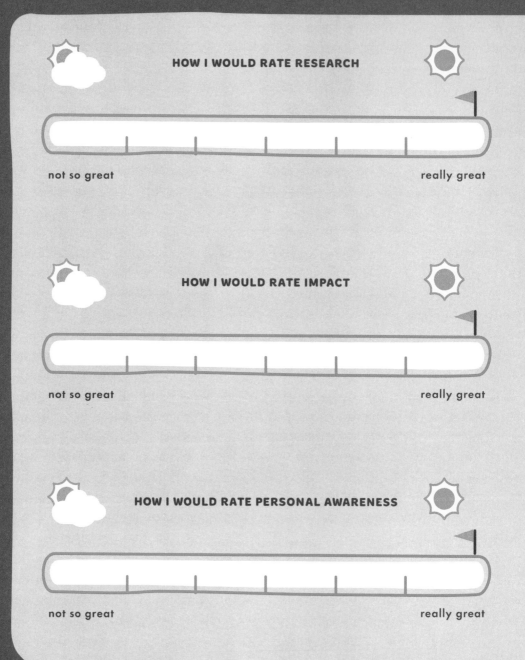

HOW I WOULD RATE RESEARCH

not so great

really great

HOW I WOULD RATE IMPACT

not so great

really great

HOW I WOULD RATE PERSONAL AWARENESS

not so great

really great

Quick CHECK-IN

SMALL WIN(S) FROM THE MONTH:

WHAT I LEARNED THIS MONTH, EITHER ABOUT A PARTICULAR ISSUE OR ABOUT MYSELF:

_____

_____

_____

_____

_____

_____

_____

_____

ROADBLOCKS I ENCOUNTERED:

HOW MY PERSPECTIVE HAS SHIFTED:

ADDITIONAL NOTES/REFLECTIONS:

Monday	Tuesday	Wednesday	Thursday

Integrity is doing the right thing even when no one is watching.
— C. S. LEWIS

Friday	Saturday	Sunday

MISSION FOR THE MONTH:

_____
_____
_____
_____
_____
_____
_____
_____

**THREE ITEMS TO RESEARCH
RELATED TO MY MISSION:**

_____
_____
_____

TASKS TO FOCUS ON:

_____
_____
_____
_____
_____
_____
_____
_____

ADVOCACY ACTION ITEMS
for the Month

Create practical action steps you plan to take to help you meet the mission you have chosen to focus on this month. Fill out as many or as few of the categories as you would like to commit to.

LOCAL

WAYS I CAN ADVOCATE WITH MY . . .
(circle one)

 Time   Talents   Resources   Voice

_____

_____

_____

NATIONAL

WAYS I CAN ADVOCATE WITH MY . . .
(circle one)

 Time   Talents   Resources   Voice

_____

_____

_____

GLOBAL

WAYS I CAN ADVOCATE WITH MY . . .

(circle one)

Time   Talents   Resources   Voice

_____

_____

_____

NOTES

_____

_____

_____

_____

_____

_____

MONTH:

_____

PEOPLE/ORGANIZATIONS
TO CONNECT WITH

○ _____

○ _____

○ _____

○ _____

○ _____

VOICES TO FOLLOW

(any authors, influencers,
organizations, politicians,
activists, etc. I already
follow or would like to learn
more about)

✖ _____

✖ _____

✖ _____

✖ _____

✖ _____

✖ _____

✖ _____

PRAYER REQUESTS

SELF-CARE

(Remember to rest and recharge.
Advocacy work can be hard!)

TO-DOS FOR EACH WEEK

NOTES

This Month's
READ/WATCH/ LISTEN LIST

MONTH:

_____

Record any media you read, watch, or listen to this month and reflect on key takeaways or quotes you would like to remember.

Date: _____ Rating: ☆ ☆ ☆ ☆ ☆

Title: _____

Source/Author: _____

What I learned: _____

_____

What surprised me: _____

_____

Memorable quote: _____

_____

Date: _____ **Rating:** ☆ ☆ ☆ ☆ ☆

Title: _____

Source/Author: _____

What I learned: _____

_____

What surprised me: _____

_____

Memorable quote: _____

_____

Date: _____ **Rating:** ☆ ☆ ☆ ☆ ☆

Title: _____

Source/Author: _____

What I learned: _____

_____

What surprised me: _____

_____

Memorable quote: _____

_____

REFLECTING on the PAST MONTH

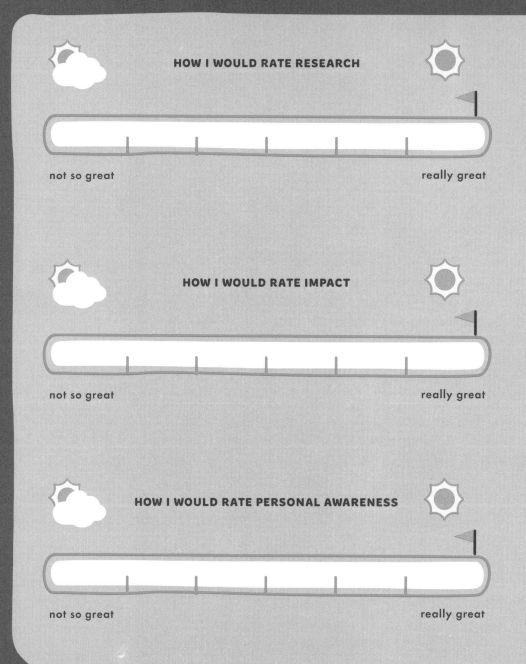

HOW I WOULD RATE RESEARCH

not so great

really great

HOW I WOULD RATE IMPACT

not so great

really great

HOW I WOULD RATE PERSONAL AWARENESS

not so great

really great

Quick
CHECK-IN

SMALL WIN(S) FROM THE MONTH:

**WHAT I LEARNED THIS MONTH,
EITHER ABOUT A PARTICULAR ISSUE
OR ABOUT MYSELF:**

ROADBLOCKS I ENCOUNTERED:

HOW MY PERSPECTIVE HAS SHIFTED:

ADDITIONAL NOTES/REFLECTIONS:

Monday	Tuesday	Wednesday	Thursday

Defend the weak and the fatherless; uphold the cause of the poor and the oppressed. — PSALM 82:3

Friday	Saturday	Sunday

MISSION FOR THE MONTH:

_____

_____

_____

_____

_____

_____

_____

THREE ITEMS TO RESEARCH RELATED TO MY MISSION:

_____

_____

_____

TASKS TO FOCUS ON:

_____

_____

_____

_____

_____

_____

_____

_____

ADVOCACY ACTION ITEMS
for the Month

Create practical action steps you plan to take to help you meet the mission you have chosen to focus on this month. Fill out as many or as few of the categories as you would like to commit to.

WAYS I CAN ADVOCATE WITH MY . . .
(circle one)

Time   Talents   Resources   Voice

_____

_____

_____

WAYS I CAN ADVOCATE WITH MY . . .
(circle one)

Time   Talents   Resources   Voice

_____

_____

_____

WAYS I CAN ADVOCATE WITH MY . . .

(circle one)

Time   Talents   Resources   Voice

_____

_____

_____

NOTES

_____

_____

_____

_____

_____

_____

MONTH:

_____

PEOPLE/ORGANIZATIONS
TO CONNECT WITH

○ ————————————————

○ ————————————————

○ ————————————————

○ ————————————————

○ ————————————————

VOICES TO FOLLOW

(any authors, influencers,
organizations, politicians,
activists, etc. I already
follow or would like to learn
more about)

✕ ————————————————

✕ ————————————————

✕ ————————————————

✕ ————————————————

✕ ————————————————

✕ ————————————————

✕ ————————————————

PRAYER REQUESTS

SELF-CARE

(Remember to rest and recharge.
Advocacy work can be hard!)

TO-DOS FOR EACH WEEK

NOTES

This Month's
READ/WATCH/ LISTEN LIST

MONTH:
_____

Record any media you read, watch, or listen to this month and reflect on key takeaways or quotes you would like to remember.

Date: _____   Rating: ☆ ☆ ☆ ☆ ☆

Title: _____

Source/Author: _____

What I learned: _____

_____

What surprised me: _____

_____

Memorable quote: _____

_____

Date: _____ Rating: ☆ ☆ ☆ ☆ ☆

Title: _____

Source/Author: _____

What I learned: _____

_____

What surprised me: _____

_____

Memorable quote: _____

_____

Date: _____ Rating: ☆ ☆ ☆ ☆ ☆

Title: _____

Source/Author: _____

What I learned: _____

_____

What surprised me: _____

_____

Memorable quote: _____

_____

REFLECTING on the PAST MONTH

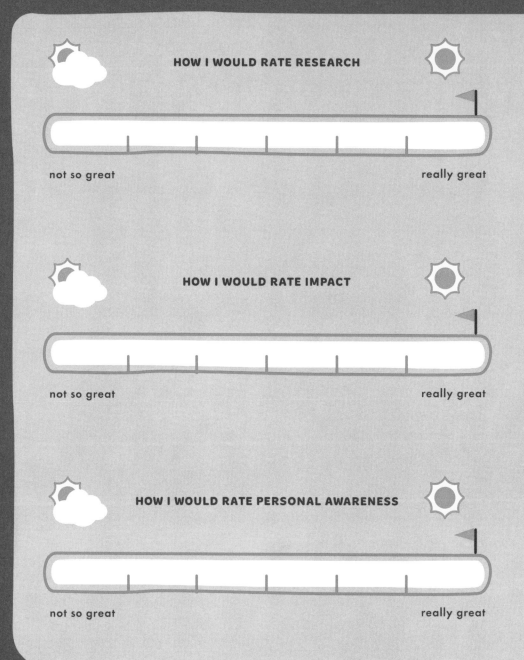

HOW I WOULD RATE RESEARCH

not so great

really great

HOW I WOULD RATE IMPACT

not so great

really great

HOW I WOULD RATE PERSONAL AWARENESS

not so great

really great

Quick CHECK-IN

SMALL WIN(S) FROM THE MONTH:

WHAT I LEARNED THIS MONTH, EITHER ABOUT A PARTICULAR ISSUE OR ABOUT MYSELF:

ROADBLOCKS I ENCOUNTERED:

HOW MY PERSPECTIVE HAS SHIFTED:

ADDITIONAL NOTES/REFLECTIONS:

Quarterly
REFLECT
& RESET

Jesus can make beauty from ashes, but the family of God must first see and acknowledge the ashes.
— LATASHA MORRISON, *BE THE BRIDGE*

HOW AM I FEELING ABOUT MY ADVOCACY?

(circle one)

IN WHAT AREAS HAVE I MADE AN IMPACT?

IN WHICH AREAS HAVE I STARTED TO FEEL BURNED OUT, OVERWHELMED, OR DISILLUSIONED?

HOW HAVE I GROWN IN MY ADVOCACY? WHERE DO I STILL HAVE ROOM TO GROW?

HOW HAVE MY OVERALL GOALS SHIFTED, CHANGED, OR BECOME STRONGER?

WHAT IS A POPULAR MISCONCEPTION I KNOW IS WRONG BUT DON'T QUITE KNOW HOW TO CONFRONT?

_____

_____

_____

_____

_____

_____

_____

WHAT IS ONE OPINION I NORMALLY WOULDN'T SHARE WITH OTHERS?

_____

_____

_____

_____

_____

_____

Name: Latasha Morrison

Champion for: racial reconciliation and justice

Organization: Be the Bridge

Publication: *Be the Bridge: Pursuing God's Heart for Racial Reconciliation* (WaterBrook, 2019)

Websites: latashamorrison.com

bethebridge.com

BIO: Latasha Morrison is a bridge-builder, reconciler, and a compelling voice in the fight for racial justice. *Ebony* magazine recognized her as one of their 2017 Power 100 for her work as a community crusader. She has spoken across the country at events that include IF:Gathering, Justice Conference, Youth Specialties, Catalyst, Orange Conference, MOPS International, and many others. In 2016 she founded Be the Bridge to inspire and equip ambassadors of racial reconciliation. In addition to equipping more than 1,000 subgroups across five countries, Be the Bridge hosts a closed, moderated online community of bridge-builders on Facebook with more than 20,000 members. Her book *Be the Bridge* was named the ECPA Christian Book of the Year for 2020.

Photo © Tomesha Faxio

THINKING
THROUGH
the PROBLEM

As you seek to make a difference in specific areas, use this creative problem-solving process to guide you in breaking down big issues into manageable action steps. This is not a linear process, and you may have to repeat certain steps to refine your ideas and make greater impact.

EMPATHIZE

How can I see from the perspective of the people affected by the issues?

DEFINE PROBLEM(S)

What are some of the underlying causes behind this issue?

BRAINSTORM SOLUTIONS

What are practical way I can make a difference (Think big/bold and small/simple.)

TAKE ACTION

How can I implement
my idea in the real
world? Who can I bring
on board to help?

GET FEEDBACK

What do others think
of my idea? Are there
any changes I can
incorporate?

PLAN STEPS

What steps can I take
to make my ideas come
o life? Who can I engage
to come alongside me?

Monday	Tuesday	Wednesday	Thursday

You may choose to look the other way but you can never again say you did not know. — WILLIAM WILBERFORCE

Friday	Saturday	Sunday

MISSION FOR THE MONTH:

_____
_____
_____

_____
_____
_____
_____

THREE ITEMS TO RESEARCH RELATED TO MY MISSION:

_____
_____
_____

TASKS TO FOCUS ON:

_____
_____
_____
_____
_____
_____
_____

ADVOCACY ACTION ITEMS
for the Month

Create practical action steps you plan to take to help you meet the mission you have chosen to focus on this month. Fill out as many or as few of the categories as you would like to commit to.

WAYS I CAN ADVOCATE WITH MY . . .
(circle one)

 Time   Talents   Resources   Voice

_____

_____

_____

WAYS I CAN ADVOCATE WITH MY . . .
(circle one)

 Time   Talents   Resources   Voice

_____

_____

_____

GLOBAL

WAYS I CAN ADVOCATE WITH MY . . .

(circle one)

Time   Talents   Resources   Voice

_____

_____

_____

NOTES

_____

_____

_____

_____

_____

_____

MONTH:

_____

PEOPLE/ORGANIZATIONS TO CONNECT WITH

○ _____

○ _____

○ _____

○ _____

○ _____

VOICES TO FOLLOW

(any authors, influencers, organizations, politicians, activists, etc. I already follow or would like to learn more about)

✗ _____

✗ _____

✗ _____

✗ _____

✗ _____

✗ _____

✗ _____

PRAYER REQUESTS

SELF-CARE

(Remember to rest and recharge. Advocacy work can be hard!)

TO-DOS FOR EACH WEEK

NOTES

This Month's
READ/WATCH/ LISTEN LIST

MONTH:

Record any media you read, watch, or listen to this month and reflect on key takeaways or quotes you would like to remember.

Date: _____   Rating: ☆ ☆ ☆ ☆ ☆

Title: _____

Source/Author: _____

What I learned: _____
_____

What surprised me: _____
_____

Memorable quote: _____
_____

Date: _____ Rating: ☆ ☆ ☆ ☆ ☆

Title: _____

Source/Author: _____

What I learned: _____

_____

What surprised me: _____

_____

Memorable quote: _____

_____

Date: _____ Rating: ☆ ☆ ☆ ☆ ☆

Title: _____

Source/Author: _____

What I learned: _____

_____

What surprised me: _____

_____

Memorable quote: _____

_____

REFLECTING on the PAST MONTH

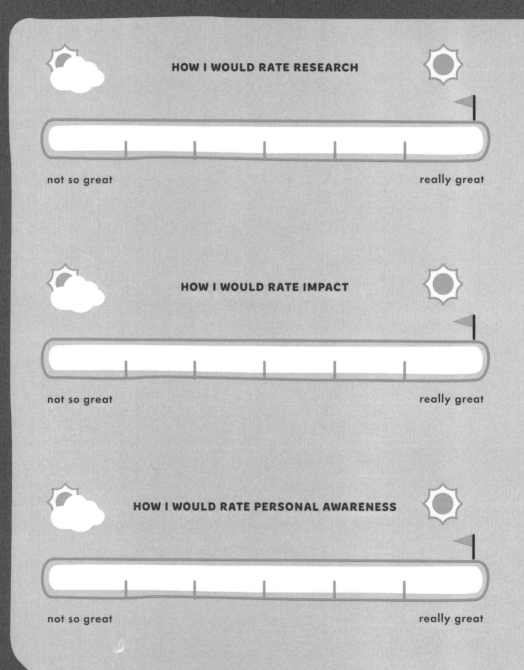

HOW I WOULD RATE RESEARCH

not so great

really great

HOW I WOULD RATE IMPACT

not so great

really great

HOW I WOULD RATE PERSONAL AWARENESS

not so great

really great

Quick CHECK-IN

SMALL WIN(S) FROM THE MONTH:

WHAT I LEARNED THIS MONTH, EITHER ABOUT A PARTICULAR ISSUE OR ABOUT MYSELF:

ROADBLOCKS I ENCOUNTERED:

HOW MY PERSPECTIVE HAS SHIFTED:

ADDITIONAL NOTES/REFLECTIONS:

Monday	Tuesday	Wednesday	Thursday

You have been a refuge for the poor, a refuge for the needy in their distress, a shelter from the storm and a shade from the heat. — ISAIAH 25:4

Friday	Saturday	Sunday

MISSION FOR THE MONTH:

_____
_____
_____
_____
_____
_____

THREE ITEMS TO RESEARCH RELATED TO MY MISSION:

_____
_____
_____

TASKS TO FOCUS ON:

_____
_____
_____
_____
_____
_____
_____

ADVOCACY ACTION ITEMS
for the Month

Create practical action steps you plan to take to help you meet the mission you have chosen to focus on this month. Fill out as many or as few of the categories as you would like to commit to.

WAYS I CAN ADVOCATE WITH MY . . .

(circle one)

 Time   Talents   Resources   Voice

_____

_____

_____

WAYS I CAN ADVOCATE WITH MY . . .

(circle one)

 Time   Talents   Resources   Voice

_____

_____

_____

WAYS I CAN ADVOCATE WITH MY . . .

(circle one)

Time   Talents   Resources   Voice

GLOBAL

_____

_____

_____

NOTES

_____

_____

_____

_____

_____

_____

MONTH:

_____

VOICES TO FOLLOW

(any authors, influencers, organizations, politicians, activists, etc. I already follow or would like to learn more about)

PEOPLE/ORGANIZATIONS TO CONNECT WITH

PRAYER REQUESTS

SELF-CARE

(Remember to rest and recharge. Advocacy work can be hard!)

TO-DOS FOR EACH WEEK

NOTES

This Month's
READ/WATCH/ LISTEN LIST

MONTH:

_____

Record any media you read, watch, or listen to this month and reflect on key takeaways or quotes you would like to remember.

Date: _____   Rating: ☆ ☆ ☆ ☆ ☆

Title: _____

Source/Author: _____

What I learned: _____

_____

_____

What surprised me: _____

_____

_____

Memorable quote: _____

_____

Date: _____ Rating: ☆ ☆ ☆ ☆ ☆

Title: _____

Source/Author: _____

What I learned: _____

_____

What surprised me: _____

_____

Memorable quote: _____

_____

Date: _____ Rating: ☆ ☆ ☆ ☆ ☆

Title: _____

Source/Author: _____

What I learned: _____

_____

What surprised me: _____

_____

Memorable quote: _____

_____

REFLECTING
on the PAST MONTH

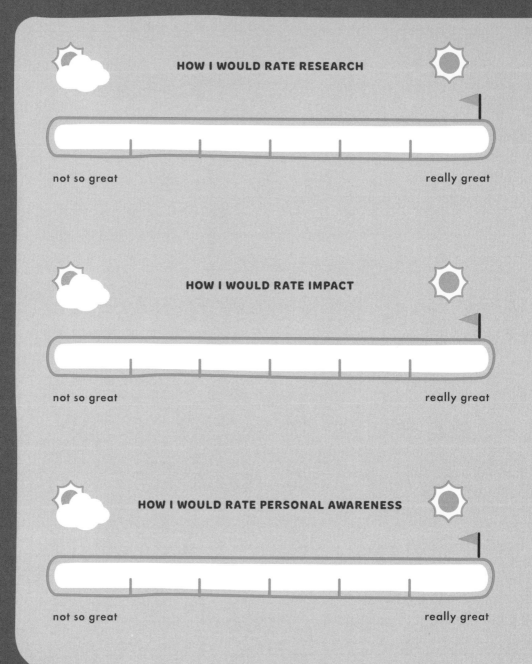

HOW I WOULD RATE RESEARCH

not so great

really great

HOW I WOULD RATE IMPACT

not so great

really great

HOW I WOULD RATE PERSONAL AWARENESS

not so great

really great

Quick CHECK-IN

SMALL WIN(S) FROM THE MONTH:

WHAT I LEARNED THIS MONTH, EITHER ABOUT A PARTICULAR ISSUE OR ABOUT MYSELF:

_____

_____

_____

_____

_____

_____

_____

ROADBLOCKS I ENCOUNTERED:

_____

_____

_____

HOW MY PERSPECTIVE HAS SHIFTED:

_____

_____

_____

ADDITIONAL NOTES/REFLECTIONS:

Monday	Tuesday	Wednesday	Thursday

erefore, as we have opportunity, let us do good to all people.
~ GALATIANS 6:10

Friday	Saturday	Sunday

MISSION FOR THE MONTH:

_____
_____
_____
_____
_____
_____

**THREE ITEMS TO RESEARCH
RELATED TO MY MISSION:**

_____
_____
_____

TASKS TO FOCUS ON:

_____
_____
_____
_____
_____
_____
_____

ADVOCACY ACTION ITEMS
for the Month

Create practical action steps you plan to take to help you meet the mission you have chosen to focus on this month. Fill out as many or as few of the categories as you would like to commit to.

WAYS I CAN ADVOCATE WITH MY . . .
(circle one)

Time   Talents   Resources   Voice

_____

_____

_____

WAYS I CAN ADVOCATE WITH MY . . .
(circle one)

Time   Talents   Resources   Voice

_____

_____

_____

GLOBAL

WAYS I CAN ADVOCATE WITH MY . . .

(circle one)

Time

Talents

Resources

Voice

_____

_____

_____

NOTES

_____

_____

_____

_____

_____

_____

MONTH:

_____

**PEOPLE/ORGANIZATIONS
TO CONNECT WITH**

VOICES TO FOLLOW

(any authors, influencers,
organizations, politicians,
activists, etc. I already
follow or would like to learn
more about)

PRAYER REQUESTS

SELF-CARE

(Remember to rest and recharge.
Advocacy work can be hard!)

TO-DOS FOR EACH WEEK

NOTES

READ/WATCH/ LISTEN LIST

MONTH:

_____

Record any media you read, watch, or listen to this month and reflect on key takeaways or quotes you would like to remember.

Date: _____   Rating: ☆ ☆ ☆ ☆ ☆

Title: _____

Source/Author: _____

What I learned: _____

_____

What surprised me: _____

_____

Memorable quote: _____

_____

Date: _____ Rating: ☆ ☆ ☆ ☆ ☆

Title: _____

Source/Author: _____

What I learned: _____

_____

What surprised me: _____

_____

Memorable quote: _____

_____

Date: _____ Rating: ☆ ☆ ☆ ☆ ☆

Title: _____

Source/Author: _____

What I learned: _____

_____

What surprised me: _____

_____

Memorable quote: _____

_____

REFLECTING
on the PAST MONTH

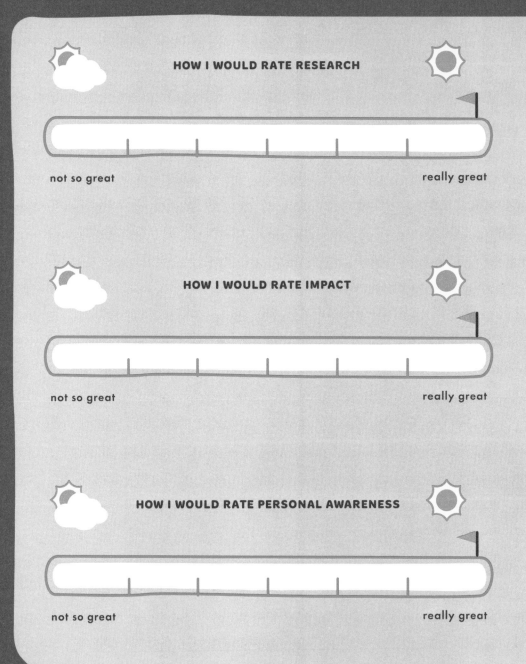

HOW I WOULD RATE RESEARCH

not so great   really great

HOW I WOULD RATE IMPACT

not so great   really great

HOW I WOULD RATE PERSONAL AWARENESS

not so great   really great

Quick CHECK-IN

SMALL WIN(S) FROM THE MONTH:

WHAT I LEARNED THIS MONTH, EITHER ABOUT A PARTICULAR ISSUE OR ABOUT MYSELF:

_____

_____

_____

_____

_____

_____

_____

_____

ROADBLOCKS I ENCOUNTERED:

HOW MY PERSPECTIVE HAS SHIFTED:

ADDITIONAL NOTES/REFLECTIONS:

Quarterly
REFLECT
& RESET

My work with the poor and the incarcerated has persuaded me that the opposite of poverty is not wealth; the opposite of poverty is justice.
—BRYAN STEVENSON

HOW AM I FEELING ABOUT MY ADVOCACY?

(circle one)

IN WHAT AREAS HAVE I MADE AN IMPACT?

IN WHICH AREAS HAVE I STARTED TO FEEL BURNED OUT, OVERWHELMED, OR DISILLUSIONED?

HOW HAVE I GROWN IN MY ADVOCACY? WHERE DO I STILL HAVE ROOM TO GROW?

HOW HAVE MY OVERALL GOALS SHIFTED, CHANGED, OR BECOME STRONGER?

Advocacy
CHALLENGE

I, _____ ,
(name)

do hereby declare that my mission for

this _____
(time period)

is to _____ the goals
(verb)

and values of _____
(organization/ministry)

in my _____ . To
(sphere of influence)

accomplish this, I will _____
(verb)

_____ , _____
(noun/person)   (verb)

_____ , and _____
(noun/person)   (verb)

by providing _____ ,
(noun/person)

advocating for _____ and
(noun)

_____ , and lending my
(noun)

support to _____ so they
(noun)

can _____ . As I uphold
(verb)

this mission, I will take care of myself by

_____ , _____
(-ing verb)   (-ing verb)

_____ , _____
(-ing verb)   (-ing verb)

and _____ . I will be held
(-ing verb)

accountable to this by _____ .
(friend or family member name)

And now, _____
(mantra or motto)

_____ !

SIGNED: _____

Advocacy
SPOTLIGHT

Name: Bryan Stevenson

Champion for: people in prison and human rights

Organization: Equal Justice Initiative (EJI)

Publication: *Just Mercy: A Story of Justice and Redemption* (Spiegel & Grau, 2014)

Website: eji.org

BIO: Bryan Stevenson, the founder and executive director of the human rights organization Equal Justice Initiative, is a widely acclaimed public interest lawyer who has dedicated his career to helping the poor, incarcerated, and condemned. He has won cases at the Supreme Court level that include the prohibition of mandatory life-imprisonment-without-parole sentences for children under seventeen as well as the protection for condemned prisoners suffering from dementia. Additionally, his organization has won relief for hundreds of prisoners who have been wrongly convicted. His bestselling and award-winning memoir *Just Mercy* was adapted into a film in 2019.[2]

THINKING THROUGH
the PROBLEM

As you seek to make a difference in specific areas, use this creative problem-solving process to guide you in breaking down big issues into manageable action steps. This is not a linear process, and you may have to repeat certain steps to refine your ideas and make greater impact.

EMPATHIZE

How can I see from the perspective of the people affected by the issues?

DEFINE PROBLEM(S)

What are some of the underlying causes behind this issue?

BRAINSTORM SOLUTIONS

What are practical ways I can make a difference? (Think big/bold and small/simple.)

TAKE ACTION

How can I implement
my idea in the real
world? Who can I bring
on board to help?

GET FEEDBACK

What do others think
of my idea? Are there
any changes I can
incorporate?

PLAN STEPS

What steps can I take
to make my ideas come
to life? Who can I engage
to come alongside me?

Monday	Tuesday	Wednesday	Thursday

The world is a dangerous place, not because of those who do evil, but because of those who look on and do nothing.
— ALBERT EINSTEIN

Friday	Saturday	Sunday

MISSION FOR THE MONTH:

_____
_____
_____
_____
_____
_____
_____

THREE ITEMS TO RESEARCH RELATED TO MY MISSION:

_____
_____
_____

TASKS TO FOCUS ON:

_____
_____
_____
_____
_____
_____
_____

ADVOCACY ACTION ITEMS
for the Month

Create practical action steps you plan to take to help you meet the mission you have chosen to focus on this month. Fill out as many or as few of the categories as you would like to commit to.

WAYS I CAN ADVOCATE WITH MY . . .

(circle one)

 Time   Talents   Resources   Voice

_____

_____

_____

WAYS I CAN ADVOCATE WITH MY . . .

(circle one)

 Time   Talents   Resources   Voice

_____

_____

_____

WAYS I CAN ADVOCATE WITH MY . . .

(circle one)

Time

Talents

Resources

Voice

_____

_____

_____

NOTES

_____

_____

_____

_____

_____

_____

MONTH:

_____

PEOPLE/ORGANIZATIONS
TO CONNECT WITH

○ _____
○ _____
○ _____
○ _____
○ _____

VOICES TO FOLLOW

(any authors, influencers,
organizations, politicians,
activists, etc. I already
follow or would like to learn
more about)

✕ _____
✕ _____
✕ _____
✕ _____
✕ _____
✕ _____
✕ _____

PRAYER REQUESTS

SELF-CARE

(Remember to rest and recharge.
Advocacy work can be hard!)

TO-DOS FOR EACH WEEK

NOTES

This Month's
READ/WATCH/ LISTEN LIST

MONTH:

_____

Record any media you read, watch, or listen to this month and reflect on key takeaways or quotes you would like to remember.

Date: _____ Rating: ☆ ☆ ☆ ☆ ☆

Title: _____

Source/Author: _____

What I learned: _____

_____

What surprised me: _____

_____

Memorable quote: _____

_____

Date: _____ Rating: ☆ ☆ ☆ ☆ ☆

Title: _____

Source/Author: _____

What I learned: _____

_____

What surprised me: _____

_____

Memorable quote: _____

_____

Date: _____ Rating: ☆ ☆ ☆ ☆ ☆

Title: _____

Source/Author: _____

What I learned: _____

_____

What surprised me: _____

_____

Memorable quote: _____

_____

REFLECTING on the PAST MONTH

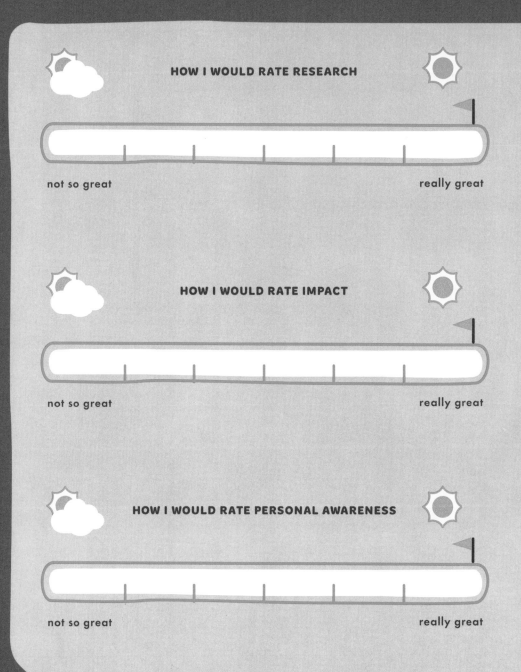

HOW I WOULD RATE RESEARCH

not so great   really great

HOW I WOULD RATE IMPACT

not so great   really great

HOW I WOULD RATE PERSONAL AWARENESS

not so great   really great

Quick CHECK-IN

SMALL WIN(S) FROM THE MONTH:

WHAT I LEARNED THIS MONTH, EITHER ABOUT A PARTICULAR ISSUE OR ABOUT MYSELF:

ROADBLOCKS I ENCOUNTERED:

HOW MY PERSPECTIVE HAS SHIFTED:

ADDITIONAL NOTES/REFLECTIONS:

Monday	Tuesday	Wednesday	Thursday

know that the Lord secures justice for the poor and upholds the
ause of the needy. — PSALM 140:12

Friday	Saturday	Sunday

MISSION FOR THE MONTH:

_____

_____

_____

_____

_____

_____

_____

**THREE ITEMS TO RESEARCH
RELATED TO MY MISSION:**

_____

_____

_____

TASKS TO FOCUS ON:

_____

_____

_____

_____

_____

_____

_____

_____

ADVOCACY ACTION ITEMS
for the Month

Create practical action steps you plan to take to help you meet the mission you have chosen to focus on this month. Fill out as many or as few of the categories as you would like to commit to.

WAYS I CAN ADVOCATE WITH MY . . .

(circle one)

Time   Talents   Resources   Voice

_____

_____

_____

WAYS I CAN ADVOCATE WITH MY . . .

(circle one)

Time   Talents   Resources   Voice

_____

_____

_____

GLOBAL

WAYS I CAN ADVOCATE WITH MY . . .

(circle one)

Time

Talents

Resources

Voice

_____

_____

_____

NOTES

_____

_____

_____

_____

_____

_____

MONTH:

_____

PEOPLE/ORGANIZATIONS TO CONNECT WITH

○ _____

○ _____

○ _____

○ _____

○ _____

VOICES TO FOLLOW

(any authors, influencers, organizations, politicians, activists, etc. I already follow or would like to learn more about)

✦ _____

✦ _____

✦ _____

✦ _____

✦ _____

✦ _____

✦ _____

PRAYER REQUESTS

SELF-CARE

(Remember to rest and recharge. Advocacy work can be hard!)

TO-DOS FOR EACH WEEK

NOTES

This Month's
READ/WATCH/ LISTEN LIST

MONTH:

_____

Record any media you read, watch, or listen to this month and reflect on key takeaways or quotes you would like to remember.

Date: _____ Rating: ☆ ☆ ☆ ☆ ☆

Title: _____

Source/Author: _____

What I learned: _____

_____

What surprised me: _____

_____

Memorable quote: _____

_____

Date: _____ Rating: ☆ ☆ ☆ ☆ ☆

Title: _____

Source/Author: _____

What I learned: _____

_____

What surprised me: _____

_____

Memorable quote: _____

_____

Date: _____ Rating: ☆ ☆ ☆ ☆ ☆

Title: _____

Source/Author: _____

What I learned: _____

_____

What surprised me: _____

_____

Memorable quote: _____

_____

REFLECTING
on the PAST MONTH

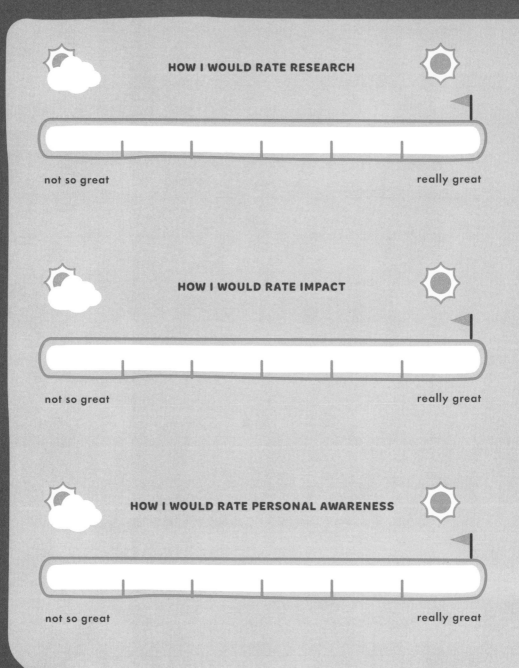

HOW I WOULD RATE RESEARCH

not so great   really great

HOW I WOULD RATE IMPACT

not so great   really great

HOW I WOULD RATE PERSONAL AWARENESS

not so great   really great

Quick CHECK-IN

SMALL WIN(S) FROM THE MONTH:

WHAT I LEARNED THIS MONTH, EITHER ABOUT A PARTICULAR ISSUE OR ABOUT MYSELF:

_____
_____
_____
_____
_____
_____
_____
_____
_____
_____

ROADBLOCKS I ENCOUNTERED:

_____
_____
_____

HOW MY PERSPECTIVE HAS SHIFTED:

_____
_____
_____

ADDITIONAL NOTES/REFLECTIONS:

Monday	Tuesday	Wednesday	Thursday

For if you remain silent at this time, relief and deliverance for the Jews will arise from another place, but you and your father's family will perish. And who knows but that you have come to your royal position for such a time as this? — ESTHER 4:14

Friday	Saturday	Sunday

MISSION FOR THE MONTH:

_____
_____
_____
_____
_____
_____
_____

THREE ITEMS TO RESEARCH RELATED TO MY MISSION:

_____
_____
_____

TASKS TO FOCUS ON:

_____
_____
_____
_____
_____
_____
_____
_____
_____

ADVOCACY ACTION ITEMS
for the Month

Create practical action steps you plan to take to help you meet the mission you have chosen to focus on this month. Fill out as many or as few of the categories as you would like to commit to.

LOCAL

WAYS I CAN ADVOCATE WITH MY . . .
(circle one)

Time   Talents   Resources   Voice

_____

_____

_____

NATIONAL

WAYS I CAN ADVOCATE WITH MY . . .
(circle one)

Time   Talents   Resources   Voice

_____

_____

_____

WAYS I CAN ADVOCATE WITH MY . . .

(circle one)

GLOBAL

Time

Talents

Resources

Voice

_____

_____

_____

NOTES

_____

_____

_____

_____

_____

_____

MONTH:

_____

PEOPLE/ORGANIZATIONS TO CONNECT WITH

○ _____

○ _____

○ _____

○ _____

○ _____

VOICES TO FOLLOW

(any authors, influencers, organizations, politicians, activists, etc. I already follow or would like to learn more about)

✖ _____

✖ _____

✖ _____

✖ _____

✖ _____

✖ _____

✖ _____

PRAYER REQUESTS

SELF-CARE

(Remember to rest and recharge. Advocacy work can be hard!)

TO-DOS FOR EACH WEEK

NOTES

This Month's
READ/WATCH/ LISTEN LIST

MONTH:

_____

Record any media you read, watch, or listen to this month and reflect on key takeaways or quotes you would like to remember.

Date: _____   Rating: ☆ ☆ ☆ ☆ ☆

Title: _____

Source/Author: _____

What I learned: _____

_____

What surprised me: _____

_____

Memorable quote: _____

_____

Date: _____ Rating: ☆ ☆ ☆ ☆ ☆

Title: _____

Source/Author: _____

What I learned: _____

_____

What surprised me: _____

_____

Memorable quote: _____

_____

Date: _____ Rating: ☆ ☆ ☆ ☆ ☆

Title: _____

Source/Author: _____

What I learned: _____

_____

What surprised me: _____

_____

Memorable quote: _____

_____

REFLECTING
on the PAST MONTH

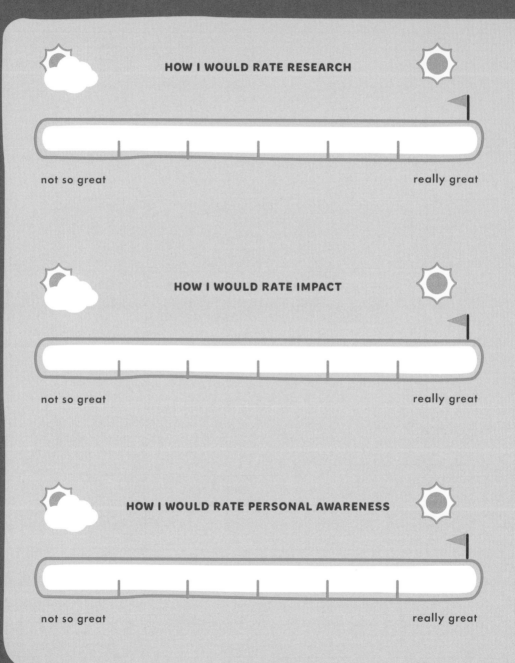

HOW I WOULD RATE RESEARCH

not so great   really great

HOW I WOULD RATE IMPACT

not so great   really great

HOW I WOULD RATE PERSONAL AWARENESS

not so great   really great

Quick CHECK-IN

SMALL WIN(S) FROM THE MONTH:

WHAT I LEARNED THIS MONTH, EITHER ABOUT A PARTICULAR ISSUE OR ABOUT MYSELF:

ROADBLOCKS I ENCOUNTERED:

HOW MY PERSPECTIVE HAS SHIFTED:

ADDITIONAL NOTES/REFLECTIONS:

Quarterly
REFLECT & RESET

When we are able to listen to someone else's story with an open heart and hear their experience, which may look different than ours, we begin to close the gap between them and us. — TERENCE LESTER

HOW AM I FEELING ABOUT MY ADVOCACY?

(circle one)

IN WHAT AREAS HAVE I MADE AN IMPACT?

IN WHICH AREAS HAVE I STARTED TO FEEL BURNED OUT, OVERWHELMED, OR DISILLUSIONED?

HOW HAVE I GROWN IN MY ADVOCACY? WHERE DO I STILL HAVE ROOM TO GROW?

HOW HAVE MY OVERALL GOALS SHIFTED, CHANGED, OR BECOME STRONGER?

Advocacy
CHALLENGE

**WHO HAS CHALLENGED OR
ENCOURAGED ME IN MY ADVOCACY,
AND HOW HAS MY RELATIONSHIP
WITH THAT PERSON CHANGED ME?**

_____

_____

_____

_____

_____

_____

**IN WHAT WAYS HAVE I BROUGHT
MY FRIENDS OR FAMILY INTO THE
CONVERSATIONS AND ISSUES
THAT MATTER TO ME?**

_____

_____

_____

_____

_____

_____

Advocacy
SPOTLIGHT

Name: Terence Lester

Champion for: eradicating systemic poverty, homelessness, and economic inequality

Organization: Love Beyond Walls

Publications: _When We Stand: The Power of Seeking Justice Together_ (2021), _I See You: How Love Opens Our Eyes to Invisible People_ (2019)

Websites: terencelester.org, lovebeyondwalls.org

BIO: Terence Lester is a speaker, author, and thought leader. In 2013, he founded the nonprofit Love Beyond Walls, whose vision is to "create a world where no one is invisible." In 2019, he founded Dignity Museum, the first museum in the US focused on changing the narratives around houselessness. His national awareness campaigns have been covered by _USA Today_, _Good Morning America_, NBC, MLK50, and CNN and have garnered international interaction and participation. In 2020, Coca-Cola named him one of its History Shakers, and American Express awarded him with the NGen Leadership Award for leaders under 40 who are "accelerating transformative social and community change."[3]

Photo © Daniela Andujo

THINKING
THROUGH
the PROBLEM

As you seek to make a difference in specific areas, use this creative problem-solving process to guide you in breaking down big issues into manageable action steps. This is not a linear process, and you may have to repeat certain steps to refine your ideas and make greater impact.

EMPATHIZE

How can I see from the perspective of the people affected by the issues?

DEFINE PROBLEM(S)

What are some of the underlying causes behind this issue?

BRAINSTORM SOLUTIONS

What are practical ways I can make a difference? (Think big/bold and small/simple.)

TAKE ACTION

How can I implement
my idea in the real
world? Who can I bring
on board to help?

GET FEEDBACK

What do others think
of my idea? Are there
any changes I can
incorporate?

PLAN STEPS

What steps can I take
to make my ideas come
to life? Who can I engage
to come alongside me?

Monday	Tuesday	Wednesday	Thursday

To me, a faith in Jesus Christ that is not aligned with the poor . . .

it's nothing. — BONO

Friday	Saturday	Sunday

This Month's
ADVOCACY GOALS

MISSION FOR THE MONTH:

_____
_____
_____
_____
_____
_____
_____

**THREE ITEMS TO RESEARCH
RELATED TO MY MISSION:**

_____
_____
_____

TASKS TO FOCUS ON:

_____
_____
_____
_____
_____
_____
_____
_____

ADVOCACY ACTION ITEMS
for the Month

Create practical action steps you plan to take to help you meet the mission you have chosen to focus on this month. Fill out as many or as few of the categories as you would like to commit to.

WAYS I CAN ADVOCATE WITH MY . . .

(circle one)

Time   Talents   Resources   Voice

_____

_____

_____

WAYS I CAN ADVOCATE WITH MY . . .

(circle one)

Time   Talents   Resources   Voice

_____

_____

_____

GLOBAL

WAYS I CAN ADVOCATE WITH MY . . .

(circle one)

Time

Talents

Resources

Voice

_____

_____

_____

NOTES

_____

_____

_____

_____

_____

_____

MONTH:

_____

**PEOPLE/ORGANIZATIONS
TO CONNECT WITH**

○ _____

○ _____

○ _____

○ _____

○ _____

VOICES TO FOLLOW

(any authors, influencers,
organizations, politicians,
activists, etc. I already
follow or would like to learn
more about)

✕ _____

✕ _____

✕ _____

✕ _____

✕ _____

✕ _____

✕ _____

PRAYER REQUESTS

SELF-CARE

(Remember to rest and recharge.
Advocacy work can be hard!)

TO-DOS FOR EACH WEEK

NOTES

This Month's
READ/WATCH/ LISTEN LIST

Record any media you read, watch, or listen to this month and reflect on key takeaways or quotes you would like to remember.

Date: _____   Rating: ☆ ☆ ☆ ☆ ☆

Title: _____

Source/Author: _____

What I learned: _____

_____

What surprised me: _____

_____

Memorable quote: _____

_____

Date: _____ Rating: ☆ ☆ ☆ ☆ ☆

Title: _____

Source/Author: _____

What I learned: _____

_____

What surprised me: _____

_____

Memorable quote: _____

_____

Date: _____ Rating: ☆ ☆ ☆ ☆ ☆

Title: _____

Source/Author: _____

What I learned: _____

_____

What surprised me: _____

_____

Memorable quote: _____

_____

REFLECTING on the PAST MONTH

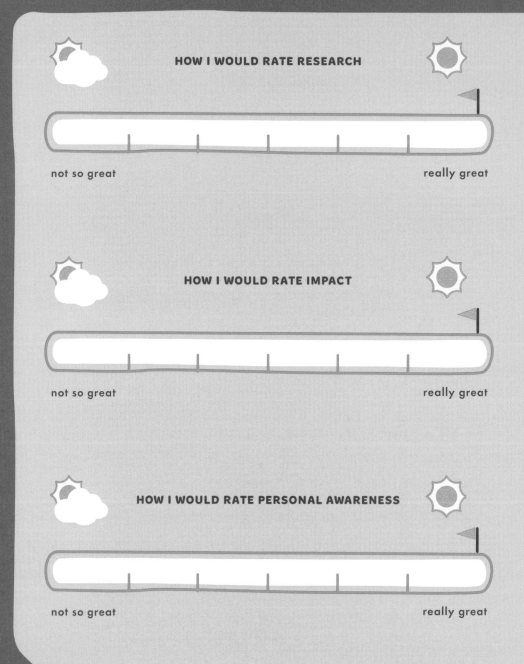

HOW I WOULD RATE RESEARCH

not so great
really great

HOW I WOULD RATE IMPACT

not so great
really great

HOW I WOULD RATE PERSONAL AWARENESS

not so great
really great

Quick CHECK-IN

SMALL WIN(S) FROM THE MONTH:

WHAT I LEARNED THIS MONTH, EITHER ABOUT A PARTICULAR ISSUE OR ABOUT MYSELF:

_____

_____

_____

_____

_____

_____

_____

_____

_____

_____

ROADBLOCKS I ENCOUNTERED:

HOW MY PERSPECTIVE HAS SHIFTED:

ADDITIONAL NOTES/REFLECTIONS:

Monday	Tuesday	Wednesday	Thursday

This is what the Lord says: Do what is just and right. Rescue from the hand of the oppressor the one who has been robbed. Do no wrong or violence to the foreigner, the fatherless or the widow, and do not shed innocent blood in this place. — JEREMIAH 22:3

Friday	Saturday	Sunday

This Month's
ADVOCACY GOALS

MISSION FOR THE MONTH:

_____

_____

_____

_____

_____

_____

_____

THREE ITEMS TO RESEARCH RELATED TO MY MISSION:

_____

_____

_____

TASKS TO FOCUS ON:

_____

_____

_____

_____

_____

_____

_____

ADVOCACY ACTION ITEMS
for the Month

Create practical action steps you plan to take to help you meet the mission you have chosen to focus on this month. Fill out as many or as few of the categories as you would like to commit to.

WAYS I CAN ADVOCATE WITH MY . . .
(circle one)

Time   Talents   Resources   Voice

_____

_____

_____

WAYS I CAN ADVOCATE WITH MY . . .
(circle one)

Time   Talents   Resources   Voice

_____

_____

_____

WAYS I CAN ADVOCATE WITH MY . . .

(circle one)

GLOBAL

Time

Talents

Resources

Voice

_____

_____

_____

NOTES

_____

_____

_____

_____

_____

_____

MONTH:

_____

**PEOPLE/ORGANIZATIONS
TO CONNECT WITH**

○ _____

○ _____

○ _____

○ _____

○ _____

VOICES TO FOLLOW

(any authors, influencers,
organizations, politicians,
activists, etc. I already
follow or would like to learn
more about)

✕ _____

✕ _____

✕ _____

✕ _____

✕ _____

✕ _____

✕ _____

PRAYER REQUESTS

SELF-CARE

(Remember to rest and recharge.
Advocacy work can be hard!)

TO-DOS FOR EACH WEEK

NOTES

This Month's
READ/WATCH/ LISTEN LIST

Record any media you read, watch, or listen to this month and reflect on key takeaways or quotes you would like to remember.

Date: _____   Rating: ☆ ☆ ☆ ☆ ☆

Title: _____

Source/Author: _____

What I learned: _____

_____

What surprised me: _____

_____

Memorable quote: _____

_____

Date: _____ Rating: ☆ ☆ ☆ ☆ ☆

Title: _____

Source/Author: _____

What I learned: _____

_____

What surprised me: _____

_____

Memorable quote: _____

_____

Date: _____ Rating: ☆ ☆ ☆ ☆ ☆

Title: _____

Source/Author: _____

What I learned: _____

_____

What surprised me: _____

_____

Memorable quote: _____

_____

REFLECTING
on the PAST MONTH

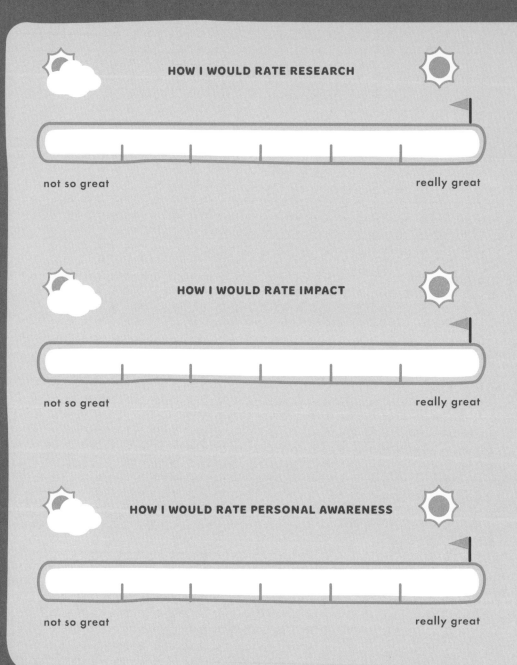

HOW I WOULD RATE RESEARCH

not so great   really great

HOW I WOULD RATE IMPACT

not so great   really great

HOW I WOULD RATE PERSONAL AWARENESS

not so great   really great

Quick
CHECK-IN

SMALL WIN(S) FROM THE MONTH:

WHAT I LEARNED THIS MONTH, EITHER ABOUT A PARTICULAR ISSUE OR ABOUT MYSELF:

ROADBLOCKS I ENCOUNTERED:

HOW MY PERSPECTIVE HAS SHIFTED:

ADDITIONAL NOTES/REFLECTIONS:

Monday	Tuesday	Wednesday	Thursday

Life's most persistent and urgent question is, "What are you doing for others?" — MARTIN LUTHER KING JR.

Friday	Saturday	Sunday

MISSION FOR THE MONTH:

_____
_____
_____
_____
_____
_____
_____

THREE ITEMS TO RESEARCH RELATED TO MY MISSION:

_____
_____
_____

TASKS TO FOCUS ON:

_____
_____
_____
_____
_____
_____
_____
_____

ADVOCACY ACTION ITEMS
for the Month

Create practical action steps you plan to take to help you meet the mission you have chosen to focus on this month. Fill out as many or as few of the categories as you would like to commit to.

WAYS I CAN ADVOCATE WITH MY . . .

(circle one)

   Time   Talents   Resources   Voice

_____

_____

_____

WAYS I CAN ADVOCATE WITH MY . . .

(circle one)

NATIONAL

 Time   Talents   Resources   Voice

_____

_____

_____

GLOBAL

WAYS I CAN ADVOCATE WITH MY . . .

(circle one)

Time

Talents

Resources

Voice

_____

_____

_____

NOTES

_____

_____

_____

_____

_____

_____

MONTH:

_____

**PEOPLE/ORGANIZATIONS
TO CONNECT WITH**

○ _____

○ _____

○ _____

○ _____

○ _____

VOICES TO FOLLOW

(any authors, influencers,
organizations, politicians,
activists, etc. I already
follow or would like to learn
more about)

✕ _____

✕ _____

✕ _____

✕ _____

✕ _____

✕ _____

✕ _____

PRAYER REQUESTS

SELF-CARE

(Remember to rest and recharge.
Advocacy work can be hard!)

TO-DOS FOR EACH WEEK

NOTES

This Month's
READ/WATCH/ LISTEN LIST

Record any media you read, watch, or listen to this month and reflect on key takeaways or quotes you would like to remember.

Date: _____ Rating: ☆ ☆ ☆ ☆ ☆

Title: _____

Source/Author: _____

What I learned: _____

_____

What surprised me: _____

_____

Memorable quote: _____

_____

Date: _____ Rating: ☆ ☆ ☆ ☆ ☆

Title: _____

Source/Author: _____

What I learned: _____

_____

What surprised me: _____

_____

Memorable quote: _____

_____

Date: _____ Rating: ☆ ☆ ☆ ☆ ☆

Title: _____

Source/Author: _____

What I learned: _____

_____

What surprised me: _____

_____

Memorable quote: _____

_____

REFLECTING on the PAST MONTH

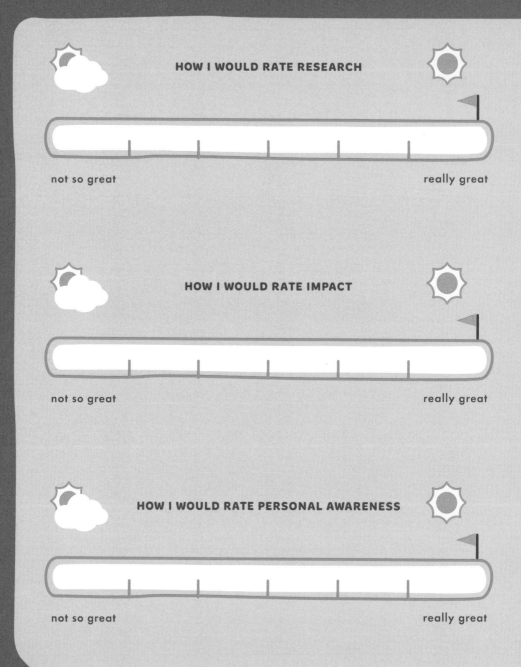

HOW I WOULD RATE RESEARCH

not so great

really great

HOW I WOULD RATE IMPACT

not so great

really great

HOW I WOULD RATE PERSONAL AWARENESS

not so great

really great

Quick CHECK-IN

SMALL WIN(S) FROM THE MONTH:

WHAT I LEARNED THIS MONTH, EITHER ABOUT A PARTICULAR ISSUE OR ABOUT MYSELF:

_____

_____

_____

_____

_____

_____

_____

_____

_____

_____

ROADBLOCKS I ENCOUNTERED:

HOW MY PERSPECTIVE HAS SHIFTED:

ADDITIONAL NOTES/REFLECTIONS:

Quarterly
REFLECT
& RESET

Give me your tired, your poor, your huddled masses yearning to breathe free. — EMMA LAZARUS

HOW AM I FEELING ABOUT MY ADVOCACY?

(circle one)

IN WHAT AREAS HAVE I MADE AN IMPACT?

IN WHICH AREAS HAVE I STARTED TO FEEL BURNED OUT, OVERWHELMED, OR DISILLUSIONED?

HOW HAVE I GROWN IN MY ADVOCACY? WHERE DO I STILL HAVE ROOM TO GROW?

HOW HAVE MY OVERALL GOALS SHIFTED, CHANGED, OR BECOME STRONGER?

WHAT IS AN ISSUE YOU THINK YOU WOULD STRUGGLE TO ADVOCATE FOR?

ISSUE:

Do a quick internet search on the issue to learn five facts or statistics about it.

1 _____

2 _____

3 _____

4 _____

5 _____

Commit to praying for a different aspect of this issue every day this week.

DAY 1	the issue
DAY 2	the people affected
DAY 3	the ministries involved
DAY 4	the leaders with agency over it
DAY 5	the circumstances or people contributing negatively to the issue
DAY 6	the hearts of those opposed to the issue
DAY 7	your own stance on the issue

Name: **Jenny Yang**

Champion for: refugee protection, immigration policy, and human rights

Organization: World Relief

Publication: *Welcoming the Stranger: Justice, Compassion and Truth in the Immigration Debate* (InterVarsity Press, 2009)

Website: worldrelief.org/leadership

BIO: Jenny Yang has been actively engaged in humanitarian work involving refugee protection, immigration, and human rights for over a decade. In her role as the senior vice president of advocacy and policy at World Relief, she acts as the ambassador for the organization's work before elected officials and also provides support and guidance to churches looking to educate and mobilize their congregations. In addition to co-authoring the book *Welcoming the Stranger* with Matthew Soerens, she has been selected to be on an active deployment roster for the United Nations High Commissioner for Refugees and is listed as one of the "50 Women to Watch" by *Christianity Today*.[4]

Photo © World Relief

THINKING
THROUGH
the PROBLEM

As you seek to make a difference in specific areas, use this creative problem-solving process to guide you in breaking down big issues into manageable action steps. This is not a linear process, and you may have to repeat certain steps to refine your ideas and make greater impact.

EMPATHIZE

How can I see from the perspective of the people affected by the issues?

DEFINE PROBLEM(S)

What are some of the underlying causes behind this issue?

BRAINSTORM SOLUTIONS

What are practical ways I can make a difference? (Think big/bold and small/simple.)

TAKE ACTION

How can I implement
my idea in the real
world? Who can I bring
on board to help?

GET FEEDBACK

What do others think
of my idea? Are there
any changes I can
incorporate?

PLAN STEPS

What steps can I take
to make my ideas come
to life? Who can I engage
to come alongside me?

ISSUES ON
GOD'S HEART

A father to the fatherless, a defender of widows,
is God in his holy dwelling.
God sets the lonely in families,
he leads out the prisoners with singing.
—PSALM 68:4–6

As the modern world marches on with ever-shifting politics, adapted ideologies, and a new digital device every year, many of us might begin to wonder whether a text as ancient as the Bible still holds cultural relevance. After all, how can we really learn from a book that was compiled during a time in history when slavery was still widely practiced, women were usually considered property, and the poor possessed virtually no rights or protections? Was the idea of "social justice" as we know it today even a consideration back then?

While it's true that the phrase "social justice" probably did not exist in common vernacular in the first century AD, the subject of caring for and sheltering the overlooked and marginalized has always been close to God's heart and a large part of His commission to us. Beginning in the Garden of Eden, God tasked Adam and Eve with shepherding the animals and tending the garden. When the Israelites left Egypt for the Promised Land, God delivered very clear instructions about how they were to treat foreigners among them, since they themselves had been strangers in Egypt. The entire book of Ruth hinges largely on the treatment of widows; and in a letter to Philemon, Paul urges his friend to treat Onesimus not as a slave, but as a brother.

Jesus's own time on earth was filled with parables on how to care for the poor or estranged, and He seemed to be always breaking tradition by spending His time with "sinners," welcoming children, and inviting women into His ministry. In one of His most pivotal sermons, He stated, "So in everything, do to others what you would have them do to you, for this sums up the Law and the Prophets" (Matthew 7:12). In other words, the entire Law can be condensed into how we treat others. As we learn in another frequently cited parable, this includes those whom we consider our neighbors . . . and even those we don't.

With this in mind, it is little wonder that so many social justice movements in history have been motivated by people who had been influenced by the ethics and principles of Christianity: Sojourner Truth, Dietrich Bonhoeffer, Mother Teresa, William Wilberforce, Florence Nightingale, Amy Carmichael, Corrie ten Boom, William Booth, Harriet Tubman, Walter Rauschenbusch, Elizabeth Fry, Robert Raikes, Rosa Parks, Martin Luther King Jr., and so many more.

In the following pages, you can read brief overviews on some of the main issues on God's heart. On each page is a list of a few organizations you can research to learn more. Please know that this selection is not exhaustive; it is merely provided to give you a starting point on your own advocacy journey.

ADOPTING AND FOSTERING

Learn to do right; seek justice. Defend the oppressed. Take up the cause of the fatherless. —ISAIAH 1:17

In the book of Matthew, we read the familiar story of how Jesus shocked His disciples and turned the established social order of the day on its head with the words, "Let the little children come to me, and do not hinder them, for the kingdom of heaven belongs to such as these" (Matthew 19:14). From this revelatory statement came untold numbers of children's songs, Sunday school murals, and picture book retellings. However, as popular as this phrase is, the message behind it is often lost or reduced to simple lip service in today's world, where millions of children still suffer neglect, abuse, or abandonment.

Several child welfare websites list staggering statistics about the conditions many children face today. Perhaps most heartbreaking is the fact that every four minutes, a child under the age of eighteen suffers some form of abuse. When it comes to those without families, of the more than 400,000 children in the United States foster care system, more than a quarter of them are waiting for adoption. Sadly, a large number of them (20,000 in 2020) will age out of the program before they can be placed with families, which often means that they will be forced to face homelessness, unemployment, or other socioeconomic challenges. In fact, three out of every ten homeless people in America were once foster kids. Furthermore, less than 3 percent of those in foster care will graduate from a higher education institution, and more than 25 percent of them will suffer from PTSD.[5]

Beyond the story listed above about Jesus's interaction with the children, the Bible includes dozens of references that highlight God's heart for neglected or orphaned children. Beginning in the Old Testament books of the prophets, Isaiah instructs Israel: "seek justice. Defend the oppressed. Take up the cause of the fatherless; plead the case of the widow" (Isaiah 1:17). In Psalms, the psalmist describes God as "a father to the fatherless" who "sets the lonely in families" (Psalm 68:5–6). Jesus embodied this trait during His time on earth, when He stated, "Whoever welcomes one such child in my name welcomes me" (Matthew 18:5). And James, the brother of Jesus, insisted that *true* religion is this: "to look after orphans and widows in their distress" (James 1:27). We might not all be called to foster or adopt, but we are all called to love and care for "the least of these," who might not be able to speak up for or defend themselves.

ADOPTING AND FOSTERING RELATED ORGANIZATIONS:

Administration for Children and Families (acf.hhs.gov), Adopt US Kids (adoptuskids.org), Alliance for Children (allforchildrenadoption.org), American Adoptions (americanadoptions.com), Annie E. Casey Foundation (aecf.org), Children's Bureau (acf.hhs.gov/cb), Casey (casey.org), Children's Rights (childrensrights.org), Child Welfare (childwelfare.gov), Dave Thomas Foundation (davethomasfoundation. org), Foster America (foster-america. org), Gladney Center for Adoption (adoptionsbygladney.com), Holt International (holtinternational.org), iFoster (ifoster.org) Love Fosters Hope (lovefostershope.org), National Council for Adoption (adoptioncouncil.org), National Foster Parent Association (nfpaonline.org), One Simple Wish (onesimplewish.org), Together We Rise (togetherwerise.org)

The earth is the LORD's, and everything in it, the world, and all who live in it; for he founded it on the seas and established it on the waters. —PSALM 24:1–2

GREEN EARTH & CLEAN WATER INITIATIVES

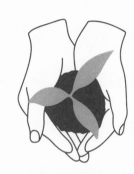

According to statistics, 785 million people—which is 1 out of every 10 people in the global population—lack the basic access to clean and hygienic drinking water. For many, that means walking for miles every day just to collect enough water for survival. This task is obviously inconvenient and even dangerous at times, but that does not dissuade the women and young girls who collectively devote up to 200 million hours a day hauling water for their families. Tragically, despite their sacrificial efforts, more than 800 children younger than the age of five are still dying every day from preventable diseases caused by contaminated water. On a larger scale, pollution, waste, and poor stewardship of the earth are leading to many humanitarian problems, such as deforestation, contaminated air, and lack of resources.[6]

Many Christians tend to be divided in their stances when it comes to conversations regarding Green Earth initiatives or eco-friendly and sustainability measures. Some might insist that others are going too far, while many believe we are simply not doing enough. However, regardless of where one may stand on the issue, we are called to take responsibility for the safety and well-being of God's creation and those who live in it. In Genesis, the first commandment we receive from God is to "fill the earth and subdue it" and to take responsibility for "the fish in the sea and the birds in the sky" (Genesis 1:28). Basically, we are to care for and tend God's beautiful creation, because it is a gift He has given us to steward (Luke 19:11–26).

More than that, creation is a reflection of God's divine nature and acts as a testimony of His Word to all who may not have heard the gospel. In Psalm 19, David describes how "the heavens declare the glory of God" and how "their voice goes out into all the earth, their words to the ends of the world" (Psalm 19:1, 4). Later, in Romans, Paul explains how creation joins with us in eagerly longing for "the glory that will be revealed." He goes on to highlight the hope creation holds that it will itself "be liberated from its bondage to decay and brought into the freedom and glory of the children of God" (Romans 8:18–21). This picture of ultimate redemption is so beautiful that it may be hard for us to acknowledge the "decay" we have to experience in the present moment. Just because we are surrounded by it doesn't mean we have to ignore it or throw up our hands in defeat. Rather, we are called to make a difference in the world God has created.

GREEN EARTH RELATED ORGANIZATIONS:

Blessed Earth (blessedearth.org), Charity Water (charitywater.org), Earth Day (earthday.org), Global Green (globalgreen.org), Life Water (lifewater. org), Living Water International (water. cc), Natural Resources Defense Council (nrdc.org), Ocean Conservancy (oceanconservancy.org), Rainforest Alliance (rainforest-alliance.org), Sierra Club (sierraclub.org), Water Mission (watermission.org), The Water Project (thewaterproject.org)

HOMELESSNESS

There will always be poor people in the land. Therefore I command you to be openhanded toward your fellow Israelites who are poor and needy in your land. —DEUTERONOMY 15:11

According to the United Nations, nearly a quarter of the world's urban population are homeless. Many of these people live without shelter or in places like slums, tents, or under bridges. Because they lack a place to call home, they also lack protection from the elements and basic sanitation needs such as toilets, sinks, and showers. Homelessness impacts families, veterans, single parents, survivors of domestic violence, the elderly, people with disabilities, individuals struggling with mental illnesses, and those living paycheck to paycheck with a fixed income—or put simply, our neighbors.

Despite common opinion that living on the streets is an active lifestyle choice, latest facts state that 25 percent of people experiencing homelessness have jobs and that one in thirty of them are under the age of eighteen. Furthermore, while many might assume people experiencing homelessness are lazy and irresponsible or have issues with addictions, the reality is that all it takes is one sudden illness, a death of a family member, unexpected unemployment, or other forces beyond one's control, and the person affected is suddenly without a home.[7]

Many of the biblical greats experienced homelessness—Moses, David, Paul, and even Jesus and His disciples. They relied on the charity and kindness of those in their community as the law commanded them to do in Leviticus 25:35: "If your brother becomes poor and cannot maintain himself with you, you shall support him as though he were a stranger and a sojourner, and he shall live with you."

The Bible also tells us that "it is a sin to despise one's neighbor, but blessed is the one who is kind to the needy" (Proverbs 14:21), and that you honor God when you "share your food with the hungry and bring the homeless poor into your house" (Isaiah 58:7, ESV). While you may not feel called to literally open your home to a person experiencing homelessness, it's important to remember that "Home goes beyond just four walls and a roof. Home is community and belonging."[8] Every person experiencing homelessness has a unique, individual story; and just like those of us blessed to have a roof over our heads, we all need shelter, security, and community. For "the rich and the poor have this in common: The LORD is the Maker of them all" (Proverbs 22:2).

HOMELESSNESS RELATED ORGANIZATIONS:

Back on My Feet (backonmyfeet.org), Beyond Housing (beyondhousing.org), Bread of Life (breadoflifemission.org), Carpenter's Shelter (carpentersshelter.org), Common Bond (commonbond.org), Community Housing Partnership (chp-sf.org), Compass Housing Alliance (compasshousingalliance.org), Congregations for the Homeless (cfhomeless.org), Council for the Homeless (councilforthehomeless.org), Covenant House (covenanthouse.org), Family Promise (familypromise.org), Habitat for Humanity (habitat.org), HomeAid (homeaid.org), I Have A Name Project (ihaveaname.org), Imagine Housing (imaginehousing.org), Love Beyond Walls (lovebeyondwalls.org), Mercy Housing (mercyhousing.org), Mobile Loaves & Fishes (mlf.org), PATH (epath.org), Plymouth Housing (plymouthhousing.org), Presbyterian Network to End Homelessness (pnteh.net), Project H.O.M.E. (projecthome.org), The Right to Shower (therighttoshower.com), Salvation Army (salvationarmyusa.org/usn/provide-shelter),The Sophia Way (sophiaway.org), Stand Up for Kids (standupforkids.org), Warren Village (warrenvillage.org)

Loose the chains of injustice and untie the cords of the yoke . . . set the oppressed free and break every yoke. —ISAIAH 58:6

HUMAN TRAFFICKING

The issue of human trafficking, which can involve any exploitative activity from prostitution or forced labor to organ harvesting, is sadly greater than many of us might care to admit. By latest counts, approximately 25 million people are being trafficked worldwide; however, many reports claim numbers as high as 40 million. The reason for this vast disparity is the simple but alarming fact that many trafficking cases go undetected. Children and teens make up more than half of these hidden figures, with females comprising the majority (about 71 percent). Each of these victims has a name, a face, and dreams of their own, but to those in the trafficking industry, they are merely another zero in the roughly $150 billion annual profit share.[9]

The phrase "human trafficking" doesn't exist anywhere in the Bible, but even without it, God's heart for the issue is abundantly clear. The Torah, or books that include the law, contains multiple stipulations that anyone who abuses, sells, rapes, or otherwise exploits another human was to be put to death. For example, Deuteronomy 24:7 (ESV) states, "If a man is found stealing one of his brothers of the people of Israel, and if he treats him as a slave or sells him, then that thief shall die. So you shall purge the evil from your midst." If there were any doubt of God's heart on the matter, Amos 2:6–7 drives the point further: "This is what the Lord says: 'For three sins of Israel, even for four, I will not relent. They sell the innocent for silver, and the needy for a pair of sandals. They trample on the heads of the poor as on the dust of the ground and deny justice to the oppressed.'"

Though slavery did exist as a cultural norm during most of biblical history and beyond, the law God gave Moses and the Israelites provided specific protections for those who were enslaved, both by promising physical safety and ensuring a time line in which slaves could eventually be freed. Furthermore, God Himself led the Israelites out of slavery in Egypt.

In the New Testament, Jesus pushed the practice of humane treatment further still by bringing a message of freedom and salvation for all. The apostle Paul summarized this message in his letter to the Galatians when he states, "There is neither Jew nor Greek, there is neither slave nor free, there is no male and female, for you are all one in Christ Jesus" (Galatians 3:28, ESV). We have all been bought with a price, and it is for freedom—not for slavery or abuse—that Christ has set us free.

HUMAN TRAFFICKING RELATED ORGANIZATIONS:

COATNET (coatnet.org), The Code (thecode.org), Destiny Rescue (destinyrescue.org), Faast International (faastinternational.org), Free the Slaves (freetheslaves.net), International Justice Mission (ijm.org), The Joseph Project (josephproject.com), Love 146 (love146.org), Mission 14 (mission14.org), National Human Trafficking Resource Center (humantraffickinghotline.org), Polaris (polarisproject.org), Priceless Ministries (pricelessministries.org), Thorn (thorn.org), World Relief (worldrelief.org)

IMMIGRATION AND REFUGEES

He executes justice for the fatherless and the widow, and loves the sojourner, giving him food and clothing. —DEUTERONOMY 10:18 (ESV)

According to the UN Refugee Agency, nearly 80 million people worldwide were forcibly displaced from their home countries in 2019 alone. The site notes that, of that number, about 26 million are refugees, "around half of whom are under the age of 18." In most cases, these are people who have been forced to flee their homes and livelihoods due to conflicts or outright persecution. Often, they end up in makeshift tent villages, where they become trapped in a sense of limbo, unable to continue the normal lives they were leading before being displaced. Even those who are not classified as refugees but claim immigrant status also experience a feeling of impermanence in an in-between space when waiting for complete settlement.[10]

Numerous organizations on both the Christian and secular sides have made it their mission to assist immigrants and refugees in the hopes of providing them shelter, food, and clothing in the immediate moment, and to defend their rights and create opportunities for their future prosperity and well-being.

Regardless of one's political opinion, these goals should align with the Christian call to be a good neighbor (Luke 10:25-37), defend the poor, and shelter the needy. The Bible's multiple references to the "foreigner," "sojourner," and "stranger" and the inclusion of Levitical laws that existed for the protection of those outside the tribe of Israel clearly reveals God's heart and compassion for those in liminal spaces. Moses urged the Israelites to remember their own status in Egypt and to treat foreigners among them with kindness and acceptance (Exodus 23:9) since they had also been foreigners in Egypt. Furthermore, Jesus Himself highlighted the importance of welcoming strangers in His parable of the sheep and the goats:

> "When did we see you a stranger and invite you in, or needing clothes and clothe you? When did we see you sick or in prison and go to visit you?"
>
> The King will reply, "Truly I tell you, whatever you did for one of the least of these brothers and sisters of mine, you did for me."
>
> **(MATTHEW 25:38–40)**

IMMIGRATION AND REFUGEE RELATED ORGANIZATIONS:

Anera (anera.org), Catholic Relief Services (crs.org), HIAS (hias.org), IRCO (irco.org/), Mercy Corps (mercycorps.org), Preemptive Love (preemptivelove.org/), Refugees International (refugeesinternational.org), Save the Children (savethechildren.org), ShelterBox (shelterboxusa.org), UNHCR (unhcr.org/en-us), UNICEF (unicef.org), We Welcome Refugees (wewelcomerefugees.com), World Relief (worldrelief.org/)

They have freely scattered their gifts to the poor, their righteousness endures forever; their horn will be lifted high in honor. —PSALM 112:9

MISSIONS AND SPONSORING

Ever since Jesus gave His disciples the Great Commission at the end of the gospel of Matthew, His followers have been "going out to all nations" with the message of salvation and the hand of healing. Even before that, at the height of Jesus's earthly ministry, He was equipping and sending His disciples to the surrounding towns with the charge to heal the sick, drive out evil spirits, and spread the news of the coming kingdom of heaven. Jesus Himself devoted all of His time on earth to a missional life of reaching the lost, welcoming the outcast, and inviting the marginalized to join Him. It is easy to see why so many Christians today jump straight to mission work when pondering how they can make a difference in the world.

MISSIONS AND SPONSORING RELATED ORGANIZATIONS:

Africa Inland Mission (aimint.org), Bethany International (bethanyinternational.org), Compassion International (compassion.com), Ethnos360 (ethnos360.org), International Mission Board (imb.org), Mission Finder (missionfinder.org), Mission Go (missiongo.org), Operation Mobilization (omusa.org), Overseas Missionary Fellowship (omf.org/us), Pioneers (pioneers.org), Samaritan's Purse (samaritanspurse.org), Send International (send.org), Team (team.org), World Vision (worldvision.org),

Missions in the Bible were further catalyzed when the church became scattered beyond Israel after the martyrdom of Stephen in the book of Acts. As house and city churches began to spread across Asia Minor, believers including Philip, Paul, Barnabas, Phoebe, Priscilla, Luke, John Mark, Euodia, Syntyche, Timothy, and others became some of the first "official" missionaries of the gospel. From their example, we can see that missionary work means not only sharing the gospel but also being the hands and feet of Jesus in very practical and service-minded ways.

Dozens of mission organizations today have long-standing, nearly century-old traditions of training, equipping, and sending missionaries to countries all around the globe. Many others partner with local churches to provide educational, medical, and spiritual support to communities. Still others dedicate their resources to planting churches, translating and distributing the Bible, or reaching the three billion people who have not yet heard the gospel.

Advocacy work of this nature might seem overwhelming or even intimidating, but for those who don't feel called to actually pick up their lives and relocate to another country to serve as missionaries, there are still many ways to get involved. Most mission organizations welcome prayer partners and monetary donations, and many offer sponsorship opportunities as well, either for those in impoverished situations or for the missionaries themselves. While some might even facilitate short-term mission trips, it is important that participants of these are mindful that these trips—whether long or short—should not be "voluntourism" for guests but life-giving partnerships with brothers and sisters across the globe who might be in need of support or healing. Bear in mind also that "missions" doesn't have to mean "international." When Jesus called us to go to all nations, chances are good He meant for us to start in our own neighborhoods.

POVERTY

The poor and needy search for water, but there is none; their tongues are parched with thirst. But I the Lord will answer them; I, the God of Israel, will not forsake them. —ISAIAH 41:17

According to a variety of sources, between 400 and 700 million people live in extreme income poverty: that's around 1 in 10 people worldwide. Furthermore, beyond forcing those affected to live in difficult conditions, poverty is also the root cause of homelessness, hunger, human trafficking, mass incarceration, racial injustice, and so many other global and national issues. Those in poverty are also more susceptible to exploitation and more vulnerable in the wake of natural disasters or national conflicts, and they often lack the means to access basic necessities for survival and personal advancement.

When we think about the poor among us, it's easy for our minds to go to a slum in Africa or India, or to think of the immigrant or the refugee. However, the reality happens to be much closer to home: one in five children in America lives in poverty in underserved communities with limited opportunities. With this in mind, we need to fight desensitization and remember the poor in our own communities—our schools, our churches, and maybe within our own families. Even if their conditions are not as extreme as those on the other side of the globe, we will "always have the poor with [us]" (Matthew 26:11, ESV), and we are called to care for them.[11]

The Bible has more than two thousand references to the poor that make it clear that the poor are close to God's heart. Many verses call them "blessed," and Proverbs 28:6 tells us, "Better is a poor man who walks in his integrity than a rich man who is crooked in his ways" (ESV). Dozens of verses also warn against the evils of exploiting the poor and point out how God will be their defender and help in those instances (Proverbs 22:22-23). Additionally, Jesus Himself lived in poverty. He gave up the riches of heaven and humbled Himself on earth for our behalf. A core piece of His mission was to "proclaim good news to the poor" (Luke 4:18).

Proverbs 19:17 states, "Whoever is kind to the poor lends to the Lord, and he will reward them for what they have done." Whether or not you're in a position to give of your own resources, even small actions like donating clothes, food, or school supplies can go a long way. However, aid is not the only way to end poverty. Investing in community development, resources, and infrastructure by supporting small businesses and donating your time or expertise can also go a long way in alleviating the grip poverty has on our neighbors, our nation, and our world.

POVERTY RELATED ORGANIZATIONS:

Alabama Possible (alabamapossible.org), Americares (americares.org), BarkerRipley (barkerripley.org), BetterAid (betteraid.org), The Borgen Project (borgenproject.org), Capital Good Fund (capitalgoodfund.org), CARE (care.org), Community-Wealthy.org (community-wealth.org), Direct Relief (directrelief.org), Ella Baker Center of Human Rights (ellabakercenter.org), End Child Poverty (endchildpovertyus.org), endPoverty (endpoverty.org), Give Directly (givedirectly.org), Global Citizen (globalcitizen.org), Institute for Research on Poverty (irp.wisc.edu), Minnesota Without Poverty (mnwithoutpoverty.org), National Urban League (nul.org), Neighborhood Partnerships (neighborhoodpartnerships.org), ONE Campaign (one.org), Oxfam (oxfamamerica.org), Poverty Solutions (poverty.umich.edu), Poverty USA (povertyusa.org), RESULTS (results.org), Robinhood Foundation (robinhood.org), Shriver Center on Poverty Law (povertylaw.org), United Way (unitedway.org), World Relief (worldrelief.org), World Vision (worldvision.org)

The Lᴏʀᴅ sets prisoners free, the Lᴏʀᴅ gives sight to the blind, the Lᴏʀᴅ lifts up those who are bowed down, the Lᴏʀᴅ loves the righteous.
—PSALM 146:7–8

PRISON REFORM AND MINISTRY

Recent data shows that the American justice system isn't exactly, well . . . just. According to the Equal Justice Initiative, false accusations are the leading causes of wrongful convictions, followed by misconduct from police or prosecutors (or both). Other issues that plague our justice system include excessive punishment, poor prison conditions, and sentencing children as young as thirteen years old to life imprisonment. There is also an imbalance of who receives punishment and who does not: nearly 70 percent of people in prison are people of color. Wherever you might stand on the issue of prison reform, it is important to remember that, while our God is a God of justice, He is first and foremost a God of redemption. With this in mind, we should be advocating for a justice that restores, not simply punishes.

With the highest incarceration rates in the world and the most wrongful convictions, the US spends around $80 billion annually on mass incarceration. And while there are programs and initiatives that support individuals during their imprisonment, few offer medical, educational, or rehabilitation support for re-entering society. Often, released individuals struggle to find housing and are burdened with court-ordered debt. Due to policy restrictions, as many as 5.2 million Americans have been banned from voting. Furthermore, with up to 60 percent of formerly incarcerated people experiencing unemployment a year after their release, it is clear how the system has created a revolving door to prison and a legacy of poverty. These challenging realities are even more sobering when considering how they also affect the nearly 10,000 people who are wrongfully convicted each year.[12]

While the Bible outlines specific consequences and punishments for wrongdoing, it also warns against biased judgments. In Leviticus 19:15 (ᴇsᴠ), God tells the Hebrews, "You shall do no injustice in court." God's heart against injustice is further highlighted in Zechariah 7:9–10 (ᴇsᴠ), when we are told to "render true judgments" and not oppress specific demographics, but instead to ensure "none of you devise evil against another."

Beyond working toward a more just system, we should also seek to minister to those in prison and those who might need comfort while a loved one is there (one in five children in the US has a parent in prison). The imprisoned often

struggle with isolation and depression due to broken community, but we as believers should not fall in with the rest of society in forgetting these people. After all, "the Lᴏʀᴅ hears the needy and does not despise his captive people" (Psalm 69:33), and we should "continue to remember those in prison as if [we] were together with them in prison, and those who are mistreated as if [we ourselves] were suffering" (Hebrews 13:3). In Matthew 25:34–40 (ᴇsᴠ), the King blesses the righteous because, "I was in prison and you came to me." Later Paul, who was often imprisoned in his lifetime, wrote, "Do not be proud, but be willing to associate with people of low position" (Romans 12:16). None of these passages dwell on the reason why someone might be in prison, but only on how we are to treat them.

RACIAL RECONCILIATION

He has shown you, O mortal, what is good. And what does the LORD require of you? To act justly and to love mercy and to walk humbly with your God. —MICAH 6:8

In the wake of the tragic events and nationwide calls for equality and justice in the last several years, the topic of racial reconciliation feels in many ways more relevant than ever. Issues and deeply felt wounds that many believed had been "handled" in the civil rights movement of the 1960s—but really had only been buried or tamped down—have again risen to the surface of societal awareness, prompting movements, conversations, and changes in long-accepted policies. As we as individuals and as a nation continue to wrestle with our own thoughts, biases, and reflexive prejudices, it is important for us to acknowledge that the legacy of slavery, internment camps, Native American genocide, segregation, and other acts that demeaned or dehumanized others can no longer be ignored or shoved under the proverbial rug. We as believers know that all are created in the image of God, and we need to start practicing what we believe.

RACIAL RECONCILIATION RELATED ORGANIZATIONS:

Be the Bridge (bethebridge.com), Congregations Organizing for Racial Reconciliation (cornnow.org), Mississippi Center for Justice (mscenterforjustice. org), Racial Justice and Unity Center (rjuc.org), Reconciliation Ministry (reconciliationministry.org), Repentance Project (repentanceproject.org), Sojourners (sojo.net/join/campaigns/ racial-justice), Southern Poverty Law Center (splcenter.org), The Witness (thewitnessbcc.com)

The Bible repeatedly teaches that all humans, regardless of their race or skin tone, deserve to be treated with dignity and respect and should be welcomed to and included within our communities. In His own ministry, Jesus made a point of crossing cultural and racial boundaries and completely refuted the established prejudices of the day by extending the good news of the kingdom of God to those outside Israel's borders. Furthermore, because He does not show favoritism, God specifically called Peter in Acts to bring the message of salvation to the Gentiles (Acts 10). So began the work that will ultimately be brought to fullness when God will gather a great multitude before Him from "every nation, tribe, people and language" (Revelation 7:9).

The gospel also speaks at length about reconciliation, not only between God and humans but also between us and our neighbors. As 2 Corinthians 5:18 reminds us, "All this is from God, who reconciled us to himself and gave us the ministry of reconciliation." As important as reconciliation is, we should be careful to remember that it cannot be forced through strength of will or the demand for forgiveness. Only through true repentance can we reach reconciliation in our hearts and in our nation. After all, "do two walk together unless they have agreed to do so?" (Amos 3:3). This is true in our relationship with God and also true in our relationship with each other.

Finally, since we are all one in Jesus Christ, we should strive to be witnesses through our love and through our ability to live at peace with one another. Even if the world continues to put up walls or appoint labels, we should be the ones leading the call for unity, equality, and justice. Our divisions might not be between Jews and Gentiles, but Paul's reminder to the Ephesians still holds true for us: "For he himself is our peace, who has made the two groups one and has destroyed the barrier, the dividing wall of hostility. . . . His purpose was to create in himself one new humanity out of the two, thus making peace" (Ephesians 2:14–15).

WORLD HUNGER

> If you spend yourselves in behalf of the hungry and satisfy the needs of the oppressed, then your light will rise in the darkness, and your night will become like the noonday. —ISAIAH 58:10

In a recent report, the UN defined *hunger* as "the term used to define periods when populations are experiencing severe food insecurity—meaning that they go for entire days without eating due to lack of money, lack of access to food, or other resources." Fortunately, ministries and organizations are daily making giant leaps in the global campaign to end this crisis. Compared to the early 1990s, there are 216 million fewer people who go to bed hungry today. However, with an estimated 800 million people still suffering from hunger or malnutrition across the globe, we still have a long way to go before we can reach a zero hunger world.

The hunger crisis currently affects nearly every corner of the globe, but there are a number of countries where the lack of food is felt more strongly, such as in Chad, North Korea, Madagascar, Liberia, Haiti, Rwanda, and Afghanistan. Furthermore, many experts have noticed a rise in numbers of those experiencing chronic hunger as a result of the COVID-19 pandemic. As an example close to home, many school-age children in the US who depended on school lunches lost access during the quarantine period to what was their one meal of the day.[13]

The Bible has a lot to say on the issue of hunger, especially when it comes to God's heart on the subject. In the Psalms, God is repeatedly praised as being the One who "fills the hungry with good things" and "[satisfies] the desires of every living thing" (Psalm 107:8–9; 145:14–16). During Jesus's earthly ministry, He warned against storing up excess for oneself and neglecting to feed the needy (Luke 12:16–21; 16:19–31). He even went so far as to say that whatever we do or don't do for others, we do to Him (Matthew 25:35–40).

James, the brother of Jesus, pushes this instruction further in his letter to the churches when he argues that true faith requires feeding and clothing the needy (James 2:15–18). And the apostle John drives the point home for all believers by writing, "But if anyone has the world's goods and sees his brother in need, yet closes his heart against him, how does God's love abide in him? Little children, let us not love in word or talk but in deed and in truth" (1 John 3:17–18, ESV).

WORLD HUNGER RELATED ORGANIZATIONS:

Action Against Hunger (actionagainsthunger.org), Bread for the World (bread.org), Feed the Hungry (feedthehungry.org), Feeding America (feedingamerica.org), Feed the Children (feedthechildren.org), Food Aid Foundation (foodaidfoundation.org), Food for the Hungry (fh.org), The Hunger Project (thp.org), No Kid Hungry (nokidhungry.org), Rise Against Hunger (riseagainsthunger.org), UN World Food Programme (wfp.org), Why Hunger (whyhunger.org), World Food Program USA (wfpusa.org), World Vision (worldvision.org)

Places
TO VISIT

Date:

_____

Location/Event:

_____

Key takeaway:

_____

_____

Rate the experience:

_____

Date:

_____

Location/Event:

_____

Key takeaway:

_____

_____

Rate the experience:

_____

NEW COMMITMENT FROM THIS EXPERIENCE:

_____

_____

_____

_____

NEW COMMITMENT FROM THIS EXPERIENCE:

_____

_____

_____

_____

List any museums, volunteer offices, monuments, landmarks, libraries, city councils, rallies, marches, etc. that you visit to learn more about a particular cause.

Date:

_____

Location/Event:

_____

Key takeaway:

_____

_____

Rate the experience:

_____

Date:

_____

Location/Event:

_____

Key takeaway:

_____

_____

Rate the experience:

_____

NEW COMMITMENT FROM THIS EXPERIENCE:

_____

_____

_____

_____

NEW COMMITMENT FROM THIS EXPERIENCE:

_____

_____

_____

_____

Places
TO VISIT

Date:

_____

Location/Event:

_____

Key takeaway:

_____

_____

Rate the experience:

_____

Date:

_____

Location/Event:

_____

Key takeaway:

_____

_____

Rate the experience:

_____

NEW COMMITMENT FROM THIS EXPERIENCE:

_____

_____

_____

_____

NEW COMMITMENT FROM THIS EXPERIENCE:

_____

_____

_____

_____

List any museums, volunteer offices, monuments, landmarks, libraries, city councils, rallies, marches, etc. that you visit to learn more about a particular cause.

Date:

Location/Event:

Key takeaway:

Rate the experience:

Date:

Location/Event:

Key takeaway:

Rate the experience:

NEW COMMITMENT FROM THIS EXPERIENCE:

NEW COMMITMENT FROM THIS EXPERIENCE:

Event
PLANNER

Use these dedicated planning pages to organize your own advocacy event, whether it's a fundraiser, a charity drive or giveaway, a bake sale, a march, or an event in your church or community to raise awareness of a particular issue.

EVENT:

PROPOSED DATE:

BUDGET:

SUPPLIES NEEDED:

VOLUNTEERS NEEDED:

TO-DO LIST

IMPORTANT NOTES OR PHONE NUMBERS:

PROJECT NAME:

EVENT SCHEDULE:

Time	Activity

Event
PLANNER

Use these dedicated planning pages to organize your own advocacy event, whether it's a fundraiser, a charity drive or giveaway, a bake sale, a march, or an event in your church or community to raise awareness of a particular issue.

EVENT:

PROPOSED DATE:

BUDGET:

TO-DO LIST

SUPPLIES NEEDED:

VOLUNTEERS NEEDED:

IMPORTANT NOTES OR PHONE NUMBERS:

PROJECT NAME:

EVENT SCHEDULE:

Time	Activity

Event
PLANNER

Use these dedicated planning pages to organize your own advocacy event, whether it's a fundraiser, a charity drive or giveaway, a bake sale, a march, or an event in your church or community to raise awareness of a particular issue.

EVENT:

PROPOSED DATE:

BUDGET:

SUPPLIES NEEDED:

VOLUNTEERS NEEDED:

TO-DO LIST

IMPORTANT NOTES OR PHONE NUMBERS:

PROJECT NAME:

EVENT SCHEDULE:

Time	Activity

Event
PLANNER

Use these dedicated planning pages to organize your own advocacy event, whether it's a fundraiser, a charity drive or giveaway, a bake sale, a march, or an event in your church or community to raise awareness of a particular issue.

EVENT:

PROPOSED DATE:

BUDGET:

SUPPLIES NEEDED:

VOLUNTEERS NEEDED:

TO-DO LIST

IMPORTANT NOTES OR PHONE NUMBERS:

PROJECT NAME:

EVENT SCHEDULE:

Time	Activity

GIVING AND DONATION *Tracker*

MONTH:

Date	Recipient	Amount	Type*

MONTH:

Date	Recipient	Amount	Type*

*Indicate whether it's a one-time donation, monthly giving, a subscription, a tithe/offering, etc.

MONTH:

Date	Recipient	Amount	Type*

MONTH:

Date	Recipient	Amount	Type*

GIVING AND DONATION *Tracker*

MONTH:

Date	Recipient	Amount	Type*

MONTH:

Date	Recipient	Amount	Type*

*Indicate whether it's a one-time donation, monthly giving, a subscription, a tithe/offering, etc.

MONTH:

Date	Recipient	Amount	Type*

MONTH:

Date	Recipient	Amount	Type*

GIVING AND DONATION *Tracker*

MONTH:

Date	Recipient	Amount	Type*

MONTH:

Date	Recipient	Amount	Type*

*Indicate whether it's a one-time donation, monthly giving, a subscription, a tithe/offering, etc.

MONTH:

Date	Recipient	Amount	Type*

MONTH:

Date	Recipient	Amount	Type*

CURRENT ELECTED OFFICIALS

Visit usa.gov/elected-officials to find the contact information for your federal, state, and local elected leaders.

FEDERAL

PRESIDENT: _____

WHITE HOUSE SWITCHBOARD: (202) 456-1414

WHITE HOUSE COMMENTS LINE: (202) 456-1111 **During Business Hours**

U.S. State Senator: _____

_____

Email: _____

Mailing Address: _____

Phone: ( ) _____

Notes: _____

U.S. State Senator: _____

_____

Email: _____

Mailing Address: _____

Phone: ( ) _____

Notes: _____

U.S. Representative: _____

_____

Email: _____

Mailing Address: _____

Phone: ( ) _____

Notes: _____

U.S. Representative: _____

_____

Email: _____

Mailing Address: _____

Phone: ( ) _____

Notes: _____

STATE

NOTES

Governor: _____
_____

Email: _____
_____

Mailing Address: _____
_____

Phone: ( ) _____

Notes: _____
_____

State Senator: _____
_____

Email: _____
_____

Mailing Address: _____
_____

Phone: ( ) _____

Notes: _____
_____

State Senator: _____
_____

Email: _____
_____

Mailing Address: _____
_____

Phone: ( ) _____

Notes: _____
_____

LOCAL

NOTES

Mayor: _____

Email: _____

_____

Mailing Address: _____

Phone: ( ) _____

Notes: _____

_____

City Council Member: _____

Email: _____

_____

Mailing Address: _____

Phone: ( ) _____

Notes: _____

_____

City Council Member: _____

Email: _____

_____

Mailing Address: _____

Phone: ( ) _____

Notes: _____

Other official: _____

_____

Email: _____

Mailing Address: _____

_____

Phone: ( ) _____

Notes: _____

_____

Other official: _____

_____

Email: _____

Mailing Address: _____

_____

Phone: ( ) _____

Notes: _____

_____

Other official: _____

_____

Email: _____

Mailing Address: _____

_____

Phone: ( ) _____

Notes: _____

_____

Other official: _____

_____

Email: _____

Mailing Address: _____

_____

Phone: ( ) _____

Notes: _____

_____

Other official: _____

_____

Email: _____

Mailing Address: _____

_____

Phone: ( ) _____

Notes: _____

_____

Other official: _____

_____

Email: _____

Mailing Address: _____

_____

Phone: ( ) _____

Notes: _____

_____

CONTACTS

Compile your advocacy network and any collaborators you encounter along the way here.

Name: _____

Email: _____

Address: _____

_____

_____

Phone: ( ) _____

Notes: _____

_____

Name: _____

Email: _____

Address: _____

_____

_____

Phone: ( ) _____

Notes: _____

_____

Name: _____

Email: _____

Address: _____

_____

_____

Phone: ( ) _____

Notes: _____

_____

Name: _____

Email: _____

Address: _____

_____

_____

Phone: ( ) _____

Notes: _____

_____

Name: _____

Email: _____

Address: _____

_____

_____

Phone: ( ) _____

Notes: _____

_____

Name: _____

Email: _____

Address: _____

_____

_____

Phone: ( ) _____

Notes: _____

_____

Name: _____

Email: _____

Address: _____

_____

_____

Phone: _(___)_____

Notes: _____

_____

Name: _____

Email: _____

Address: _____

_____

_____

Phone: _(___)_____

Notes: _____

_____

Name: _____

Email: _____

Address: _____

_____

_____

Phone: _(___)_____

Notes: _____

_____

Name: _____

Email: _____

Address: _____

_____

_____

Phone: _(___)_____

Notes: _____

_____

Name: _____

Email: _____

Address: _____

_____

_____

Phone: _(___)_____

Notes: _____

_____

Name: _____

Email: _____

Address: _____

_____

_____

Phone: _(___)_____

Notes: _____

_____

Name:

Email:

Address:

Phone: ( )

Notes:

Name:

Email:

Address:

Phone: ( )

Notes:

Name:

Email:

Address:

Phone: ( )

Notes:

Name:

Email:

Address:

Phone: ( )

Notes:

Name:

Email:

Address:

Phone: ( )

Notes:

Name:

Email:

Address:

Phone: ( )

Notes:

Name: _____

Email: _____

Address: _____

_____

_____

Phone: ___( )_____

Notes: _____

_____

Name: _____

Email: _____

Address: _____

_____

_____

Phone: ___( )_____

Notes: _____

_____

Name: _____

Email: _____

Address: _____

_____

_____

Phone: ___( )_____

Notes: _____

_____

Name: _____

Email: _____

Address: _____

_____

_____

Phone: ___( )_____

Notes: _____

_____

Name: _____

Email: _____

Address: _____

_____

Phone: ___( )_____

Notes: _____

_____

Name: _____

Email: _____

Address: _____

_____

Phone: ___( )_____

Notes: _____

NOTES

1. waterbrookmultnomah.com/books/592177/be-the-bridge-by-latasha-morrison-foreword-by-daniel-hill-afterword-by-jennie-allen.

2. eji.org/bryan-stevenson.

3. terencelester.org/about.

4. worldrelief.org/leadership.

5. Statistics provided in "Adopting and Fostering" are from adoptionnetwork.com/adoption-myths-facts/domestic-us-statistics, americanadoptions.com, togetherwerise.org/foster-care-awareness-month, and foster-america.org.

6. Statistics provided in "Green Earth and Clean Water Initiatives" are from worldvision.org/clean-water-news-stories/global-water-crisis-facts, thewaterproject.org/why-water/water-crisis, and lifewater.org/water-crisis.

7. Statistics provided in "Homelessness" are from undocs.org/A/73/310/rev.1 and sophiaway.org/homelessness-myths-and-facts.

8. jamieivey.com/hh344.

9. Statistics provided in "Human Trafficking" are from dosomething.org/us/facts/11-facts-about-human-trafficking#fn2, humantraffickinghotline.org, ijm.org/slavery, and unodc.org/unodc/data-and-analysis/glotip.html.

10. Statistics provided in "Immigration and Refugees" are from unhcr.org/en-us/figures-at-a-glance.html.

11. Statistics provided in "Poverty" are from globalcitizen.org/en/categories/defeat-poverty, endpoverty.org/poverty-today, and endchildpovertyus.org/our-kids-our-future.

12. Statistics provided in "Prison Reform and Ministry" are from eji.org/criminal-justice-reform/ and sentencingproject.org.

13. Statistics provided in "World Hunger" are from actionagainsthunger.org/world-hunger-facts-statistics, un.org/en/global-issues/food, worldvision.org/hunger-news-stories/world-hunger-facts#:~:text=How%20many%20people%20are%20hungry,exceed%20840%20million%20by%20 2030, actionagainsthunger.org/world-hunger-facts-statistics, and foodaidfoundation.org/world-hunger-statistics.html.